KU-228-430

# ClothDollWorkshop

BEVERLY MASSACHUSETTS

From the Beginning and Beyond
with Doll Masters
*elinor peace bailey, Patti Medaris Culea,*
*and Barbara Willis*

QUARRY BOOKS

© 2010 by Quarry Books

All rights reserved. No part of this book may be reproduced in any form without written permission of the copyright owners. However, the publisher grants permission for the purchaser of this book to copy the patterns for personal use. All images in this book have been reproduced with the knowledge and prior consent of the artists concerned, and no responsibility is accepted by the producer, publisher, or printer for any infringement of copyright or otherwise, arising from the contents of this publication. Every effort has been made to ensure that credits accurately comply with information supplied. We apologize for any inaccuracies that may have occurred and will resolve inaccurate or missing information in a subsequent reprinting of the book.

First published in the United States of America by
Quarry Books, a member of
Quayside Publishing Group
100 Cummings Center
Suite 406-L
Beverly, Massachusetts 01915-6101
Telephone: (978) 282-9590
Fax: (978) 283-2742
www.quarrybooks.com

**Library of Congress Cataloging-in-Publication Data**
Bailey, Elinor Peace.
  Cloth doll workshop from the beginning and beyond with doll masters Elinor Peace Bailey, Patti Medaris Culea, and Barbara Willis / Elinor Peace Bailey, Patti Medaris Culea, and Barbara Willis.
    p. cm.
  Includes index.
  ISBN 978-1-59253-621-4
1. Dollmaking. I. Title.
  TT175.B3237 2011
  745.592'21--dc22

                                        2010020458

ISBN-13: 978-1-59253-621-4
ISBN-10: 1-59253-621-2

10 9 8 7 6 5 4 3 2 1

Design: Laura H. Couallier, Laura Herrmann Design
Photography by: Isaac Bailey Photography, pages 2–11, 13, 14, 20–42, 90–95; Courtesy of BerninaUSA.com, 14; Robert Hirsch, 12, 15, 43–65, 69–89, 96–107, 125; Barbara Willis, 64, 67
Technical Editor: Beth Baumgartel
Illustrations: Judy Love
Templates: elinor peace bailey

Printed in Singapore

**KENT LIBRARIES AND ARCHIVES**

| C333006743 | |
|---|---|
| **Askews** | |
| | |
| | |

# Cloth Doll Workshop

1

C333006743

QUARRY

# Dedication

We dedicate this book to friendship
and the creative process.

# Contents

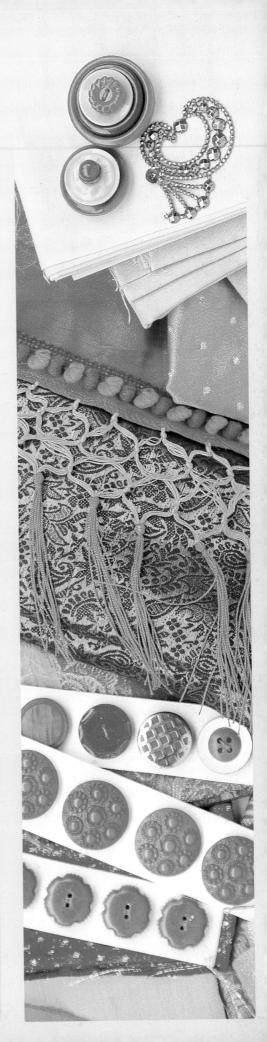

# Introduction

Patti Culea, elinor peace bailey, and Barbara Willis, three well-loved and respected doll-making friends invite you to join them in their studios as they teach the art of doll making, from beginning and beyond. You'll see where their own dolls are born and how they embrace the more challenging aspects of jointing and costuming. Your three tutors are nationally known for their individual styles and teaching techniques. They want to share with you how to create a basic cloth doll and much of what they have learned over the years.

## elinor peace bailey

To make a basic pancake doll, elinor peace bailey provides all the patterns and knowledge you need. You'll be able to garner a multitude of different looks through small changes in fabrics and easy-to-sew clothing. Then, she'll show you how to create second and third generations of the same basic doll by disengaging parts and reassembling them with different joints; you'll be able to create completely different-looking dolls.

# Patti Medaris Culea

gets you started with a simple doll body and head. After that, look out! She'll show you how to make your doll spectacular with fabrics, trims, and easy embellishments. Because Patti has a special love and understanding for drawing and coloring faces, her focus on the face will help bring life, light, and dimension to a flat surface. From there, she'll show you how changing a few body parts gives shape to the torso and hands, how simple wiring of the fingers creates movement and interest, and how to recycle a child's old sweater into a fabulous doll vest. Patti closes her adventure with you by sharing several interpretations of dolls she has made from the patterns included in this book using all kinds of materials; this will give you even more inspiration and ideas.

# Barbara Willis

wishes to engage you not only in basic cloth doll making but several elementary design possibilities as well. You'll use basic sewing machine skills—a straight stitch and a narrow zigzag—that's all. More importantly, she teaches the importance of embracing the learning curve and enjoying the whole doll-making experience, including the ups and the downs. Barbara insists that what might be considered mistakes are nothing more than the precursors to excellence and are worthy exercises.

Barbara's trio of dolls is simple, yet sophisticated, showcasing a slightly less traditional approach. For each doll, the lower part is flat with three-dimensional elements; its design falls somewhere between flat and fully dimensional, so it should appeal to doll makers of all skill levels: the new doll maker because it's rather simple, the intermediate doll maker because of the design possibilities, and the more advanced doll maker because of its unique concept. You'll be amazed at how simple changes make significant differences in the overall look of the finished dolls.

# CHAPTER 1

# Getting Started

This is a brief overview and guide to the materials and supplies used in the creative art of doll making and in this book. While each designer has her own unique and personal style, they all agree about the merits of 100 percent cotton fabric, the importance of embellishments, and the satisfaction of working with basic and novelty sewing and crafting tools.

*A custom tool holder, made of fabric, by elinor peace bailey.*

# Fabrics, Threads, and Embellishments

## FABRIC

Fundamental to all cloth dolls is good quality fabric. All of the designers recommend 100 percent cotton fabric for the doll's body, particularly the face and hands. Cotton doesn't stretch—it's easy to manage, keeps its shape, and provides a nice smooth finish for facial features. Choose from a wide variety of flesh colors for the head, face, arms, and hands. Often the torso and legs are made in decorative fabrics, such as printed cotton and silk dupioni to emulate clothing.

Barbara believes woven Pima cotton is a good choice for its sooth, silk-like hand. Patti likes working with 100 percent cotton batik; it has a high thread count, so it doesn't fray as easily as loosely woven fabrics. The batik dye process causes the colors to puddle, creating a realistic flesh look. Another batik advantage is that the fabric has just enough wax left in it to facilitate turning small body parts, such as the fingers, right-side out. And elinor agrees that 100 percent cotton flesh-colored fabric is ideal for the body parts and wants to remind you to choose your favorite from a wide variety of different skin tones.

Although silk does fray more than cotton, it can be used as long as you allow for wider seam allowances; it's perfect for the torso and legs, or to make the doll costumes. Silk dupioni has color depth and richness and sews up beautifully. Avoid substituting synthetic fabrics for the silk or cotton since they don't hold up or stitch as well, especially for the body parts of the dolls.

## •••• TIP

Don't restrict yourself to fabric yardage that you buy off the bolt. The local thrift store is one of elinor's favorite places to shop for fabric. A child's striped T-shirt made perfect leg warmers for her latest doll.

## A Word about Color

Color sets the mood and the stage for your doll. Use colors that you love and that make you happy. Barbara loves a soft vintage color palette; Patti often chooses bright, vibrant and graphic colors and patterns; while elinor's combination of colors and patterns is most certainly modern and bold. You are sure to have your own ideas of the magic of color, and that is where your own creative spirit begins. The dolls in this book are tremendous reference for the mixing and use of color; use them as a jumping-off point for your personal color statement.

## Peltex

Peltex, made by Pellon, is a brand of heavyweight nonwoven material used to stiffen a project. It comes in fusible and nonfusible varieties. There are similar products from other manufacturers that are suitable substitutes; but, note whether you need the fusible or nonfusible type.

# THREAD

A regular, sewing-weight polyester or cotton-wrapped polyester thread is the best choice for most doll making projects as it has extra strength that 100 percent cotton thread does not have. The pressure of the stuffing will sometimes pop seams open if the thread is not strong enough.

Decorative threads, such as rayons and metallics, can be used to embellish your doll's costume, but shouldn't be used to construct the body of the doll. You'll also need heavy, nylon upholstery thread, or button and craft thread for joining doll body parts and other hand sewing that requires a strong thread. Nymo and C-Lon are strong enough for both sculpting and joining body parts.

# EMBELLISHMENTS

For inspiration, start a collection of trims and embellishments. Keep even the smallest scraps and remember that dyeing is always an option. Fill your trim box with laces, doilies, ribbons, beads, buttons, braids, edgings, insertions, and specialty fabrics. Shop home décor departments, scrapbook supply stores, and flea markets for unusual embellishments. You'll find goodies at thrift stores and garage sales; remember, doll making shouldn't be expensive.

# STUFFING

A good grade of fiberfill is as important as good quality fabric. Stuffing comes in several grades and varieties. A fast compacting stuffing wads easily; however, it tends to form bumps. Fiberfill with a silicone finish has a slippery feel that doesn't compact as quickly and tends to meld into the existing stuffing, instead of forming lumps or bumps.

 TIP

The authors recommend Fairfield's Soft Touch Supreme and Fairfield's Polyfil stuffing for the best texture on stuffed body parts.

# Supplies

Gather your supplies before you begin your project. The supplies listed in the "Basic Doll-Making Supply Kit" are fairly standard and are most likely already in your sewing toolbox.

## •••• TIP

Disappearing or fade-away ink pens are useful for marking facial features and stitching lines. Barbara especially recommends the purple fade-away marker with a regular tip (not the micro or small tip) because the marks fade away completely, and the color doesn't migrate to other parts of the doll.

## BASIC DOLL-MAKING SUPPLY KIT

- sewing machine capable of zigzag stitch
- sewing machine needles in a variety of sizes
- open toe ¼" (6 mm) appliqué presser foot
- iron, ironing board, and press cloth
- straight pins and hand-sewing needles
- ruler
- paper and fabric scissors
- mechanical pencil
- disappearing or fade-away fabric marking pens
- straight-nose hemostats
- seam ripper
- ⅛" (3 mm) hole punch
- heavy nylon upholstery thread for attaching arms and legs
- polyester or cotton-wrapped polyester thread

# SPECIFIC DOLL-MAKING AND FACE-PAINTING SUPPLIES

More specific to making the dolls in this book are permanent ink markers, gel pens, colored pencils, stuffing forks, and turning tubes, all of which are important and helpful tools.

- stuffing forks
- turning tubes
- Turn-it-All
- permanent ink pens in black, brown, red, and colors for eyes (005 or the larger 01 tip)
- white, light blue, and green gel pens for coloring the eyes
- white acrylic paint and a small brush
- colored pencils for coloring the lips, eyes, and cheeks
- powdered eye shadows and blushes
- short liner brush for eye shadow application
- hair fibers
- fiberfill
- spray art fixative (such as Krylon Workable Fixative)

Stuffing forks (see "Resources", page 123) come in two sizes. The mini stuffing fork is used to stuff fingers, and the regular size is used to stuff torsos and limbs. A Turn-it-All is similar but primarily used for turning limbs and slim body parts, instead of the hands.

Permanent inks pens, colored pencils, gel pens, and makeup are the tools you use to create the doll's faces. Always test the pens on an area of the doll that won't show, such as the back of the doll's head. There are many brands of pens, most of which are suitable as long as the tip is no larger than 01. An 005 tip is an excellent drawing pen because the tip is so small and it is ideal for drawing delicate features; however, it's often only available on the Internet. Scrapbook stores are a good source for gel pens and permanent archival ink pens.

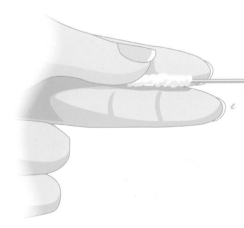

*Lay the mini stuffing fork in the ditch between your two fingers, over the stuffing. Hold the fork with your thumb. Rotate the fork around and around evenly in one direction. The fork will grab and load a long, even tube of stuffing.*

# Working with the Patterns

Copy all the pattern pieces (pages 108–122) for the doll you plan to make onto cardstock paper at a copy center. The patterns provide a wealth of information regarding layout, openings, and stitching. If the pattern needs to be enlarged, it will be indicated on the pattern and can be done at the copy store at the same time.

Carefully cut out the copied patterns to create templates that you can use over and over again. Each designer has slightly different ways of working with the pattern templates, so refer to the section for the doll you intend to make for more information. You will notice that Patti's and elinor's doll patterns usually include seam allowances, which are indicated by the dotted lines inside the solid lines. Barbara's patterns, however, do not include seam allowance, so it is important that after tracing the templates onto the fabric that you don't cut the fabric directly on the traced lines. Also, be sure to punch out the holes indicated on Barbara's feature-template guide with a ⅛" (3 mm) punch. General instructions follow.

1. Fold the fabric in half with the right sides together.

2. Position the pattern templates on the fabric, taking care to note the grainlines. If the pattern has an arrow drawn on it, then the pattern should be positioned with the arrow on the straight grain of the fabric, which is parallel to the finished or selvage edge of the fabric.

## •••• TIP

It is important to follow the grainline arrow to ensure that the fabric stretches as needed for a particular body part. For instance, the head pattern pieces are almost always positioned with the arrow along the straight grain so that the cheeks will fill out as you stuff them, creating a nice plump face.

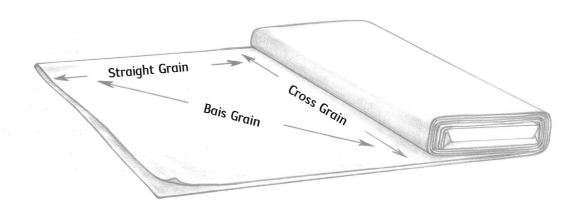

Straight Grain

Bais Grain

Cross Grain

# Marking and Stitching

**3.** Lightly trace around the templates with a mechanical pencil directly on the folded fabric. If you are working with dark fabric, trace the templates with a light color gel pen or a colored pencil that can be seen on the fabric.

**4.** For Patti's and elinor's doll patterns, you can cut the fabric directly on the outside (cutting lines) after you have traced the templates onto the fabric. The stitching lines are indicated with a dashed line, ¼" (6 mm) from the cutting lines. For some of Patti's patterns, you'll need to sew one seam before cutting around the remainder of the pattern

For Barbara's doll patterns, **don't** cut the fabric on the marked lines; they are the stitching lines. You will be sewing directly on the traced lines unless otherwise noted. Instead, rough cut around the marked lines leaving about 2" (5.1 cm) all around. After sewing, cut out the doll pieces about ¼" (6 mm) outside the seams to create the seam allowance. If you're working with silk, allow for a slightly larger seam allowances to prevent blown-out seams.

## MARKING

If you want to transfer stitching guidelines, attachment points, or facial features from the template to the fabric, use a purple fade-away marker or a mechanical pencil. The ink from the fade-away marker may take a few days to disappear, but it eventually does. Barbara swears by her purple fade-away marker! Patti draws her facial features with a light touch and a mechanical pencil. Once she is satisfied with her face, she goes over the pencil marks with a permanent ink pen and then simply erases any remaining pencil marks.

## SEWING

It is always a good idea to start a new project with a new sewing machine needle. An open-toe presser foot allows you to see your traced stitching lines as you stitch, which is the key to better accuracy.

Most doll making is done on a sewing machine with either a straight or zigzag stitch. Set the stitch length between 1.5 and 2 (14 to 16 stitches per inch or 2.5 cm), depending on the size of the stitching area. Smaller body parts, such as the face and hands, benefit from the shortest stitch, while the torso and legs can be sewn with a slightly longer stitch. These short stitch lengths will help prevent the seams from popping open.

The seam allowance ranges from a scant ⅛" (3 mm), to a standard ¼" (6 mm) wider or to a scant ½" (1.3 cm) depending on the detail and the type of fabric. The smaller the body part, the narrower the seam allowance should be. Working with silk or fabric that frays is the only time you'll need wider seam allowances. Bulk in the seam makes it harder to turn a doll casing or appendage right side out. Curved seam allowances require clipping up to, but not through, the stitching line. Clipping is especially important for the hands and fingers and between scallops on some of the clothing. Clipping helps an inward curve bend easily and an outward curve appear less wrinkled.

## Hand Stitching Guide

There are several hand stitches that are used throughout the book. It is also important to know how to bury the thread tails to make the doll stronger and more attractive.

### Bury the Thread Tails

After securing a closure with a knot, insert the needle and thread back into the fabric next to the knot, pulling the knot inside to bury the thread tails in the doll body. Bring the needle back out of the doll opposite the entry point and trim the threads close to the body so they aren't visible.

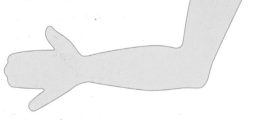

### Ladder Stitch or Slipstitch

Use this stitch to join two fabrics together along the fabric folds. Form the stitches directly across from each other and through the fabric folds so they aren't visible on the right side.

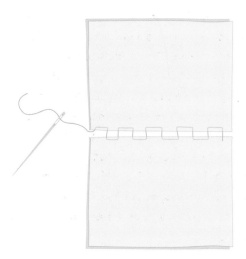

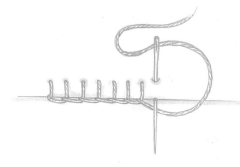

### Running Stitch (above)

This straight stitch is used to attach trim, to hem, or to gather. Use short stitches for permanent sewing and widely spaced stitches for gathering.

### Blanket Stitch

This decorative stitch is used to finish an edge or attach an appliqué. Work from left to right and insert the needle the desired distance from the fabric edge. Hold the thread behind the point of the needle and pull the needle through the fabric and over the thread to form a knot at the fabric edge. Repeat, making sure your stitches are evenly spaced.

### Whipstitch

This stitch, similar to an overcast stitch, is used to decoratively join two fabric edges or to prevent a cut edge from raveling. Simply form diagonal stitches over the cut edge(s) with stitches as deep and as close together as desired.

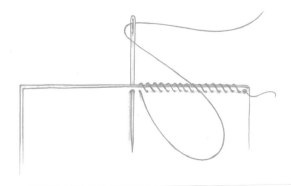

# Turning and Stuffing

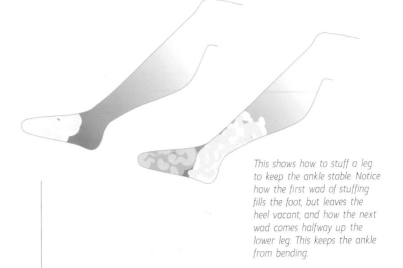

*This shows how to stuff a leg to keep the ankle stable. Notice how the first wad of stuffing fills the foot, but leaves the heel vacant, and how the next wad comes halfway up the lower leg. This keeps the ankle from bending.*

Turning the body parts right side out and stuffing them are two very important steps. Smooth seams, defined fingers, and a lump-free doll are fundamental. Here are a few guidelines to help.

## TURNING

Some of the body parts, particularly the hands and fingers, are very small and can be difficult to turn right side out smoothly and without bursting the seams open. Turning tubes (see "Resources", page 123) make turning a little easier.

To use the tubes, insert the larger tube inside a finger (or thumb). Then using the smaller tube, turn over the seam allowance, and press against the finger. The pressure against the seam allowance will help push the finger inside the hand. Then with the thumb and index finger, pull the fabric onto the smaller tube.

You'll need two hands, so hold the larger tube against your stomach. After you turn each finger, reach in with your hemostats and turn the hand and then the arm right-side out.

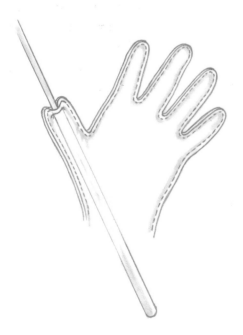

## STUFFING

The torso, arms, and legs are stuffed quite firm. For stuffing all the body parts except the hands, grab as much stuffing as can fit through the opening. Larger bunches of stuffing give a smooth look, while smaller bunches can look lumpy. Use a regular size stuffing fork or a blunt end pair of straight-nose hemostats to help you compact the stuffing so the limbs and torso are stuffed firmly.

Use the mini stuffing fork (see page 15), to stuff the fingers. Often the fingers and hands are wired, so you need only minimal amounts of stuffing positioned on top of the wires near the top of the fingers. After the fingers are stuffed, you can lightly stuff the top and palm of the hand using the hemostats. Be careful not to overfill the hands, use just enough stuffing to sandwich and encase the wires.

After the limbs and torso are stuffed, spray them with a fine mist of water or spray starch. Place a pressing cloth or a paper towel over each piece, and then press and steam each one carefully. No need to press hard just let the steam and weight of the iron do the work for you. Then set the body parts aside to dry. This will give a lovely finished texture to the limbs and torso. By flattening the torso you'll get rid of lumps, bumps and wrinkles as long as you have stuffed firmly. This also works miracles on the neck portion of the upper torso.

# elinor peace bailey

LIKE ALL CRAFT MOVEMENTS, THE COMMUNAL MAKING OF cloth dolls has a history. I shall begin my history lesson at the point when I entered "stage left" at the International Quilt Market in 1983. This is where I met Virginia Robertson of Osage County Quilt Factory (now Robertson Enterprises). She was the only doll maker in attendance and she reached out to me. Virginia taught me everything I needed to know about making and publishing patterns. More importantly, she taught me that by opening doors for another, you allow what you have to flow through you, trusting that as you let go of what you have gathered, it will be restored to you many times over.

I spent the next several years reaching out to others who knew about dolls and doll publications and where doll making was happening. I discovered the growing doll making world among the quilters at the International Quilt Market and started teaching the craft myself. I encouraged my students who showed powerful, individual style to teach others and to develop patterns. All that I had learned, I taught. Many of my students and fellow doll makers became my dearest friends and companions. We team taught; we attended and supported doll conferences; we became creative partners, and fostered doll making clubs.

The women whom I join in this book endeavor are two of those dear friends. I first met Patti in class, then I saw her fabulous work at the Manteca Doll Show in Manteca, California, at which I was a judge. She won, of course. Patti was also at the first Doll University in 1991 in San Jose, California, which was run by Judy Watersin.

Barbara crossed my path in San Jose at a local quilt shop. She was then and still is so gifted. We both knew she could create her own audience. She knows how to create "pretty" better than any cloth doll maker I know.

Patti, Barbara, and I see the doll very differently. We focus on totally different things. We gather different things. We have personal signatures. We have become companions. We love each other's work. Competition would create paucity; cooperation produces abundance. It's that simple. Now we want to share with you. Come along and join us for the giggle.

## ELINOR'S STUDIO

A visit to elinor's studio reveals an exercise in quiet encroachment. She has pretty much taken over the family area and grudgingly shares the couch and a bit of a table with her long-suffering sister Marie Fay. "If you can't see it, what's the use of having it?" elinor asks. She insists on seeing her full palette of trims, fabric, buttons and beads. Chaos reigns during the creative process; however, restoring order helps elinor refocus. She also loves containers and drawers, which seem like small revelations.

# Getting Started

Ginger, our first doll project together, is a simple pancake doll with only two pattern pieces: the body and the legs. The second doll (page 32), named Gypsy, has an additional five pattern pieces that allow the limbs to bend and take different positions. Both dolls have additional pattern pieces for their clothing.

## PREPARE THE PATTERNS

All of the pattern pieces include seam allowances and have important reference markings on them. Copy the pattern pieces on pages 108–112 onto heavy paper or card stock and cut them out. Several pattern pieces have appliqués, such as the blouse, undershirt sleeves, upper tights, and lower tights printed on them. Trace the appliqués onto lightweight paper and then onto card stock to create patterns for each of them. Refer to the cutting list for each doll or to the patterns for cutting instructions.

## ···· TIP

To create an entire upper-body pattern from the half pattern given, fold a piece of lightweight paper in half, position the paper fold on the solid line of the pattern, and copy all the markings onto the paper. Copy the appliqué markings as well. Cut along the outside line through both layers. Unfold the paper for a whole Upper Body Pattern.

# Making Ginger

## MATERIALS LIST

- basic doll-making supply kit (page 14)
- specific doll-making and face-painting supplies list (page 15)
- $^3/_8$ yard (34.3 cm) flesh-colored body fabric
- $^1/_4$ yard (22.9 cm) shirt fabric
- $^1/_4$ yard (22.9 cm) tights and cuff fabric
- cotton scraps for under sleeves, peplum, yoyos
- $^1/_4$ yard (22.9 cm) each of two colors of tulle for skirting
- scrap of T-shirt knit—cut into two 3" (7.6 cm) squares for the socks
- silk scraps for the vest
- three 10" (25.4 cm) lengths of ribbon
- one charm for the neck ribbon
- three black buttons for vest
- black beads to trim the vest
- beads for earrings
- sequins and beads for top tulle skirting
- wool yarn for hair
- matching threads, sewing, button, and craft threads
- #7 long darners
- beading needle
- Fairfield Poly-fil
- silver or gold Lumiere paint and glitter for shoes
- gesso (a primer for the paint on the shoes)
- Crayola crayons

## CUT THE FABRICS

You can cut all the fabrics that you need before you get started because the seam allowance is included in the patterns. Here is a cutting list so you don't forget anything.

### CUTTING LIST

- Body, Blouse appliqué, and Upper tights appliqué: Cut 2 each with the solid line positioned on the straight-grain fabric fold.
- Legs: Cut 4 times on cross-grain of the fabric.
- Lower tights and Undershirt sleeve appliqués: Cut 4 times.
- Vest (Use pattern included with Gypsy.): Cut 1 from fabric and 1 from lining with solid line positioned on the straight-grain fabric fold.
- Peplum: Cut 1 from fabric and 1 from lining.
- Yoyos: Cut 2 from same fabric as peplum.
- Pant cuffs: Cut 4 from same fabric as lower leg appliqués.
- Leg warmers: Cut 2 squares 3" (7.6 cm) each.
- Tulle overskirts: Cut a 45" × 9" (114.3 × 22.9 cm) underskirt and a 45" × 7" (114.3 × 17.8 cm) overskirt.

**1.** Fold the flesh-colored fabric in half lengthwise, and position the Upper Body pattern on the fabric fold. Pin the pattern in place, and cut out the upper body. Remove the pattern and cut a second upper body piece. (A)

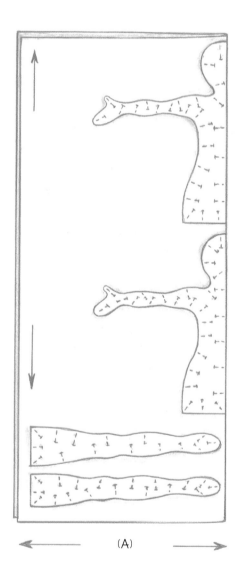

(A)

**2.** Position the Leg pattern on the cross grain. Pin and cut out the legs. Repeat so you have four fabric leg pieces.

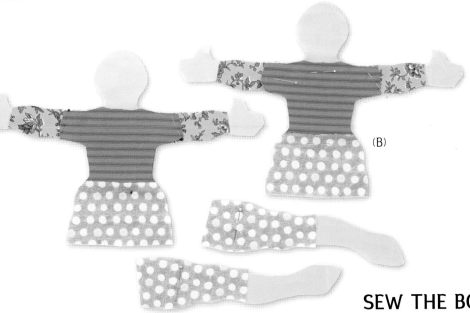

(B)

## SEW THE BODY

**3.** Pin the traced appliqué pattern pieces to their selected fabrics. Lay out the cut appliqué fabrics on the doll body to make sure they fit and look right. Allow about ¼" (6 mm) of extra fabric to underlap the edges of the undershirt sleeves and the upper edge of the upper tights. Cut out the appliqués; they provide a way of dressing the doll before it is made, so you don't have to make itsy-bitsy doll clothes. **(B)**

**4.** Cut the clothing fabrics as indicated in the cutting list (opposite) for the vest, peplum, yoyos, pants cuff, leg warmers, and overskirt. **(C)**

**1.** Staystitch the appliqués to the body and legs at the edges. Refer to the patterns for placement. Stitch over the raw edges of the appliqués with a zigzag stitch. **(D)**

(D)

**2.** With the right sides facing, pin and stitch the two body pieces together, leaving an opening at the lower edge. Repeat for the leg pieces, leaving the top edges open. Clip the seam allowances as needed for smooth, even seams. Turn the body and legs right-side out. Turning tubes (page 19) make turning small body parts easier. **(E)**

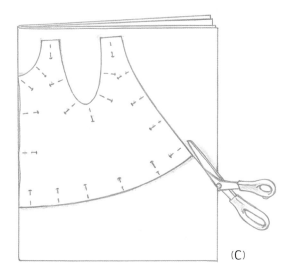

(C)

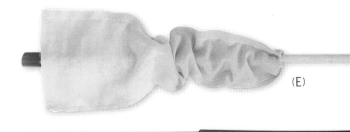

(E)

## SEW THE BODY (continued)

**3.** Stuff the legs; refer to page 19 for stuffing instructions. Minimize or reduce the amount of stuffing near the top of each leg. Topstitch the legs closed.

**4.** Pin the top edge of the two legs to the lower edge of the body with the cut edges aligned. Topstitch the legs to one layer of the body fabric. **(F)**

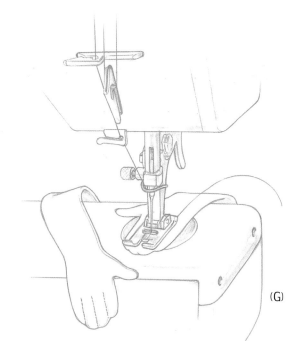

(G)

**5.** Stuff the upper body beginning with the hands. Stuff the hands lightly, and before stuffing the arms, topstitch the hands to create the fingers. Stitch the centerline first and then the lines on either side. **(G)**

**6.** Add stuffing up to the elbows, and then topstitch across each arm at the wrist to form a joint; refer to the pattern for the topstitching location. Stuff the upper arm, and then stitch across the arm at the shoulder. Stuff the remainder of the body firmly. Pin the crotch opening closed and hand work a ladder stitch (page 18) to close the opening. Knot and then bury the threads (page 18). **(H)**

(F)

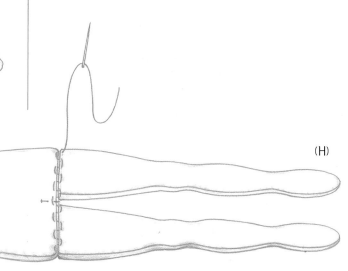

(H)

# DRESS AND FINISH GINGER

**1.** With the right sides of the vest and lining fabrics together, stitch the vest as indicated, leaving a break in the stitching. Clip the curved sections of the seam allowance, and then turn the vest right-side out and press. Close the opening by hand with the ladder stitch (page 18). (I)

(I)

**2.** Use a beading needle and beading thread to stitch the beads along the curved bottom of the vest ¼" (6 mm) apart. Overlap the shoulder tabs from the back to the front and stitch a black button through both layers on each shoulder. Slip the vest on the doll body and hold it in place at the center front with a third button. (J)

(J)

**3.** Paint the feet with gesso, and let it dry. Then paint a layer of Lumiere paint over the gesso, sprinkle the wet paint with glitter, and let the feet dry.

**4.** With the right sides of two cuff pieces together, stitch around the outside of the circle; repeat with remaining two pieces. Turn the cuffs right-side out and press. Press under the raw edges of the inside circle, and then slide the cuffs over the shoes to the bottom of the tights; slipstitch or ladder stitch (page 18) them in place.

**5.** To make the leg warmers, fold each 3" (7.6 cm) square of knit with the right sides together, and stitch the edges opposite the fold to make two tubes. Turn the tubes right-side out and slide them over the ankles just over the shoes.

**6.** Sew the shorter sides of each piece of tulle together with a hand needle and the blanket stitch to make two tubes. Layer the two pieces of tulle with the smaller piece on top. Using the heavy button thread, hand sew gathering stitches at the waist. Slide the tulle skirt onto the doll. Pull the gathers tight, tie the threads in a knot, and tack it at the waist with the seams at the center back. The peplum will cover the gathers. Sew an assortment of sequins and beads randomly over the tulle skirt.

## DRESS AND FINISH GINGER
### (continued)

**7.** A peplum is a bit of skirting that is usually attached to the waist of a jacket. You created a faux jacket with the appliqué on the doll's body. The peplum will be three-dimensional. With the right sides together, stitch the lining to the peplum fabric, leaving it open as indicated. Clip the seam allowance and turn the peplum right-side out. Press and stitch the peplum closed by hand. Tack the peplum in place at the doll's waist.

**8.** With the right side of the yoyo fabric facing up, fold over a tiny hem and stitch around that hem with a knotted button thread and #7 long darner. (a) Draw the stitches together to gather up the yoyo and bring the needle to the back of the yoyo through the center. (b) Pull and tie off the thread. (c)

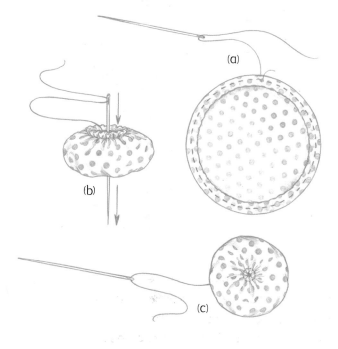

(a)

(b)

(c)

**9.** Hand stitch the two yoyos to the front of the peplum.

**10.** Refer to the illustration to draw the face on the doll. Begin by marking the eye locations with straight pins. (K)

(K)

**11.** If you feel a little insecure about drawing the features, work with a light colored pencil. Once you are happy with them, go over the pencil markings with a fine tipped permanent-marking pen. (L)

(L)

## TIP

I use .03 Permawriter II in
brown by Yasutomo & Co.
to draw doll faces.

(a)

(b)

(c)

(d)

**12.** Next, add color with brush-tipped fabric pens, colored pencils, and Crayola crayons. Finish with a soft fabric paint to add the whites of the eyes and any highlights. (M)

(M)

(N)

**13.** To wig your doll, wrap yarn over four fingers twelve times. (a) Slip the yarn off your fingers and tie a thread around the center of the yarns; pull the thread tight and secure it with an overcast knot. (b) Trim the ends, since this doll likes short hair. (c) Repeat to make two more hair sections. Tack the knotted fibers on the top of the head. (d) Again, trim the yarn. Is she fabulous or what?

**14.** Hand sew beads or charms to the sides of Ginger's head to make earrings as shown in the photograph. Sew the charm in the center of one of the 10" (25.4 cm) ribbon pieces. Tie all the 10" (25.4 cm) ribbons on top of each other around Ginger's neck to make a necklace. (N)

Approximate size 25" (64.8 cm)

# Making Gypsy

Gypsy is similar to Ginger in her simplicity, but with the addition of five pattern pieces she can sit, cross her legs and wave her arms. Patterns for the Upper Arm, Lower Arm, Upper Leg, and Lower Leg, which will be connected with a flange joint, are provided. The fifth pattern piece—the gusset, which will be added to the bottom of the body to expand its shape—will need to be created using the stuffed body as the template. The gusset will allow the doll to sit, and the flange joints will allow the limbs to bend and take positions.

Additionally Gypsy has a dart in her toes that will make her feet three-dimensional. You'll also learn several costuming tricks, including tubes for sleeves and pantaloons, a braid for wigging rather than yarn tufts, and trims and findings that wonderfully enhance the costuming possibilities.

## PREPARE THE PATTERNS

Copy Gypsy's Body, Upper Arm, Lower Arm, Upper Leg, Lower Leg, Vest, Vest Ruffle, and Overskirt pattern pieces (on pages 110–112) onto heavy paper and cut them out. The pattern pieces include seam allowances, and the body has the blouse and tights appliqués printed on them. Trace the appliqués onto lightweight paper to create patterns for each of them.

## MATERIALS LIST

- basic doll making supply kit (page 14)
- specific doll-making and face-painting supplies list (page 15)
- ³/₈ yard (34.3 cm) flesh colored body fabric
- ¹/₈ yard (11.4 cm) black fabric for legs and shoes
- (20" × 10") (50.8 × 25.4 cm) lace remnant (long edge should be finished for bloomers)
- ¹/₈ yard (11.4 cm) flamboyant woven cotton blouse print
- ¹/₄ yard (22.9 cm) each for overskirt and lining
- ¹/₄ yard (22.9 cm) for skirt and ruffle
- 1¹/₄ yards (1 m) metallic trim for skirt ruffle
- ¹/₂ yard (45.7 cm) trim for blouse sleeves
- ¹/₄ yard (22.9 cm) of 1¹/₂" (8.8 cm) -wide lace trim for blouse sleeves
- ¹/₂ yard (45.7 cm) satin ribbon for belt
- jewelry finding for a buckle
- silk scraps for vest
- 8" (20.3 cm) tasseled scarf or handkerchief for head scarf
- beads, and bits of old jewelry for necklace and earrings
- beading needle
- #7 long darners
- matching threads for fabric and buttons
- about 12 yards (11 m) of knitting yarn for hair
- Fairfield Poly-fil
- 2 buttons for vest

## CUT THE FABRICS

Again, you can cut all the fabrics that you need before you get started because the seam allowances are included in the patterns. Here is a cutting list so you don't forget anything.

## CUTTING LIST

- Body, Blouse appliqué, and Tights appliqué: Cut 2 of each with the solid line positioned on the straight-grain fabric fold.

- Upper legs and Lower legs: Cut 4 each from black fabric.

- Upper arm and Lower arm: Cut four each from flesh-colored fabric.

- Vest and Vest ruffle: Cut 1 from fabric and 1 from lining with solid line positioned on the straight-grain fabric fold.

- Tights appliqué: Cut 2 on fabric fold from black lace and black backing fabric.

- Gusset (see "Sew the Body, Appliqués and Some Clothes," step 4): Cut 1 from black lace and 1 from black backing fabric.

- Bloomers: Cut 2 pieces of lace, each 10" (25.4 cm) square.

- Sleeves: Cut 2 pieces of blouse fabric, each 5" (12.7 cm) square.

- Yoyos (Use pattern included with Ginger): Cut 4 from blouse fabric.

- Overskirt: Cut 2 from overskirt fabric using the pattern.

- Skirt: Cut 1 piece (5½" × 22½" [14 × 57.2 cm]) from desired fabric.

- Skirt ruffle: Cut 1 piece (1¾" × 45" [4.4 × 114.5 cm]) from desired fabric.

**1.** Layer two pieces of the flesh-colored fabric, and then fold them in half lengthwise with the straight grain running along the fold. Pin the Upper-Body pattern on the fabric fold and trace. Cut out along the marking, and you'll have two whole upper bodies when you unfold the fabric. **(A)**

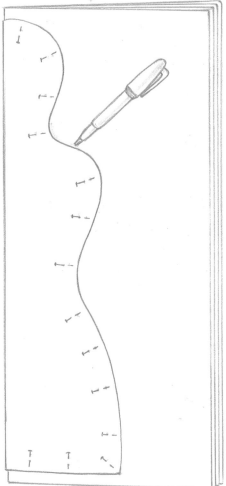

(A)

**2.** Fold the flesh-colored fabric in half with the right sides together, and trace the Upper arm and Lower arm patterns two times each. Cut them out.

**3.** Fold the black fabric in half with the right sides together, and trace the Upper leg and Lower leg patterns two times each. Cut them out.

**4.** Pin the traced appliqué pattern pieces on to their own selected fabrics. Allow about ¼" (6 mm) of extra fabric for an underlap at the top edge of the tights appliqué. Cut out the appliqués; they provide a way of dressing the doll before it is made, so you don't have to make itsy-bitsy doll clothes.

**5.** Cut the clothing fabrics as indicated in the cutting list (opposite) and the sewing instructions below.

## SEW THE BODY, APPLIQUÉS, AND SOME CLOTHES

**1.** Staystitch the appliqué edges to the body. Refer to the patterns for placement. (B)

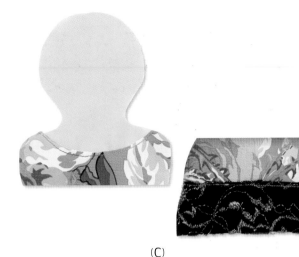

(C)

**2.** Cover the raw edge of the appliqué at the neckline and top of the tights by top-stitching the trim of your choice in place. (C)

**3.** With the right sides facing, pin and stitch the two body pieces together with a very short stitch, leaving the bottom unstitched. Clip the curved seams and turn the body right-side out.

**4.** To make the gusset pattern, lightly stuff the bottom of the doll to the desired shape. Trace around the bottom of the doll and then add ¼" (6 mm) all around for a seam allowance. Cut out the gusset pattern and then cut the gusset from black fabric and lace fabric. Baste the two layers together. Remove the stuffing so you can stitch the gusset to the body.

(B)

## SEW THE BODY, APPLIQUÉS,
## AND SOME CLOTHES (continued)

**5.** With right sides together, stitch the gusset to the back half of the lower body edge, beginning and ending at the side seams. Stuff the body (page 17) and set it aside. (D)

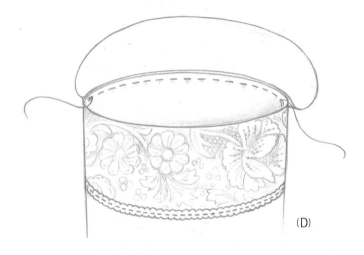

(D)

**6.** With the right sides facing, stitch the upper legs together and the lower legs together as indicated on the patterns. Set the lower legs aside. Clip, turn and stuff the upper legs. Reduce the amount of stuffing as you near the top of the legs. Press and stitch the top edges together. (E)

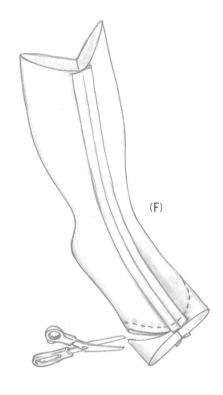

(F)

**7.** To shape the toes of the lower legs, press the two seams together at the toe opening. Stitch an arc-shaped seam across the toe. Trim the excess fabric. (F)

**8.** With the lower legs still wrong-side out, press the two seams at the top of each lower leg together to form a U-shape. Stitch across each top edge, leaving an opening at the center of the U-shape so you can turn the legs right-side out as show in the photograph below. Clip the curved seam allowances, turn the lower legs right-side out, and stuff the legs firmly. (G)

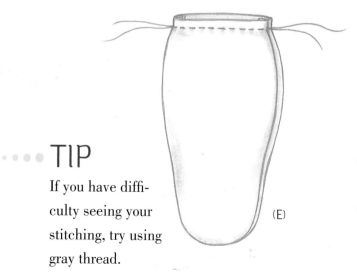

(E)

## TIP

If you have difficulty seeing your stitching, try using gray thread.

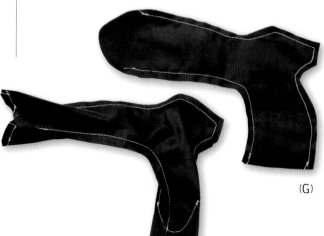

(G)

9. Stitch closed the lower legs with a hand-sewing needle and thread. Knot the thread and begin stitching at the seam in the center of the "U." Stitch across one side to the tip of the joint. Repeat to close the other side. Tie off and bury the thread.

10. To join the upper and lower legs together, use a heavy thread and long needle. Knot the thread and insert the needle so the knot is at the back of the leg and a few threads over from the previous thread. Insert the needle through the lower-leg flange, through the knee of the upper leg, and then through the remaining flange. Repeat until the joint is securely in place. Knot off, bury, and clip the thread (page 18). (H)

• • • • TIP

If the lace you have chosen doesn't have a finished edge, topstitch a piece of lace trim to one long edge.

11. The bloomers are made from two 10" (25.4 cm) squares of black lace. Fold each piece of lace in half to form a tube with the finished edge positioned at the lower tube opening; stitch the seam. Turn the tubes right-side out and hand-sew gathering stitches at the top unfinished edge. Slip the bloomers over the legs and pull the gathers at the top edge so the bloomers are snug to the top of the upper legs. Tie off the threads. Staystitch the gathered lace to the leg.

12. Pin the upper legs to the front of the doll body so the cut edges are aligned; stitch. (The photo below shows how this is done on Ginger.) Stuff the doll body firmly, especially at the neck. Pin and hand stitch the bottom closed, using the ladder stitch. Set the body aside. (I)

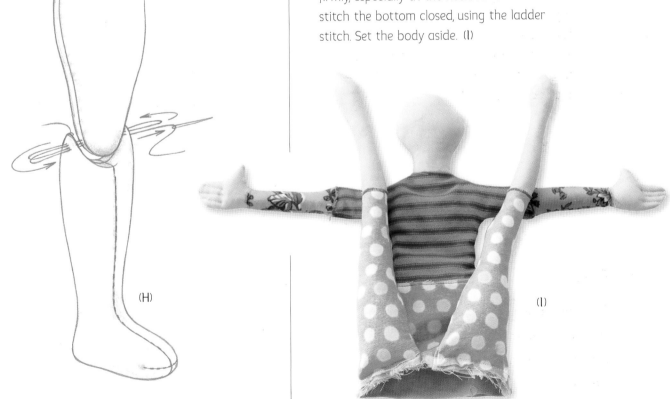

(H)

(I)

## SEW THE BODY, APPLIQUÉS, AND SOME CLOTHES (continued)

**13.** A tab joint made from the flesh-colored fabric and the blouse fabric will be used to attach the arms to the body. Cut a piece of each fabric 1" × 2" (2.5 × 5.1 cm). (a) With the right sides together, stitch the two pieces together along the 2" (5.1 cm) side, and press the seam open. (b) Cut this piece in half, across the seam. (c) Fold each 1" × 2" (2.5 × 5.1 cm) piece in half lengthwise, with the right sides together. Stitch them along one short edge and the long edge, as shown. (d) Turn the ½" × 2" (1.3 × 5.1 cm) tabs right-side out, fold the raw edges in, stitch them closed and set aside. (e)

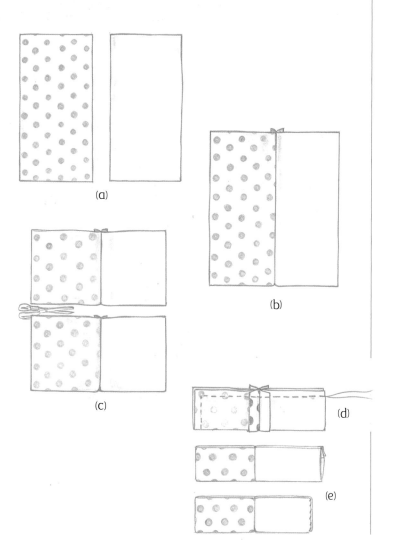

(a)

(b)

(c)

(d)

(e)

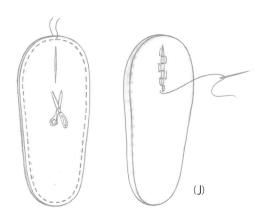

(J)

**14.** With the right sides together, stitch the upper arms. The shoulders will be a little wider than the elbows. Make a small slash as indicated on the pattern piece through one fabric layer. Use the slashed opening to turn the upper arms right-side out. Stuff the arms, and close the slashed openings with the ladder stitch. (J)

**15.** Hand stitch the flesh end of a tab joint over the slash stitching on each upper arm. Fold the tabs back on themselves, and then pin the blouse ends to the body at the shoulders. Use the ladder stitch to join the tabs all the way around, including the folded edge, to the body. (K)

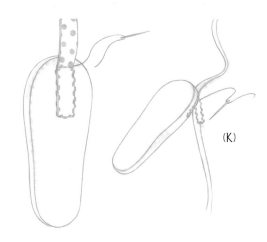

(K)

**16.** With the right sides together, stitch the lower arm, leaving it open where the pattern indicates. With the arm still wrong-side out press the two seams together at the top of the elbow, so the top of the lower arm forms a U-shape. Stitch across the top of the arm, leaving an opening at the center of the "U." Clip the seam allowance in the curved area, turn the arm right-side out, and stuff the hand lightly. Repeat for the other lower arm.

**17.** Topstitch the fingers starting at the center stitching line, and then sew the two remaining stitching lines. Continue stuffing the lower arm firmly. To close the joint by hand, start the ladder stitch at the seam in the center of the joint and then stitch to the tips at each side of the joint. Tie off and bury the thread. Don't forget to paint her nails!

**18.** With a new, knotted thread, insert the needle so the knot is at the outside of the arm (with the thumb pointing toward the front of the body) and a few threads over from the previous thread. Insert the needle through the flange, then through the elbow of the upper arm, and through the remaining flange. Repeat until the joint is securely in place. Knot off, bury, and clip the thread. Sew buttons to each side directly over the stitching. **(L)**

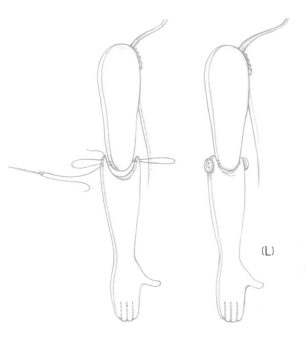

(L)

## DRESS AND FINISH GYPSY

**1.** Press a ¹/₂" (1.3 cm) hem on one edge of each sleeve piece so the right sides are together. Stitch the 1¹/₂" (3.8 cm) -wide pregathered lace on the upturned hems and then topstitch trim over the seams. **(M)**

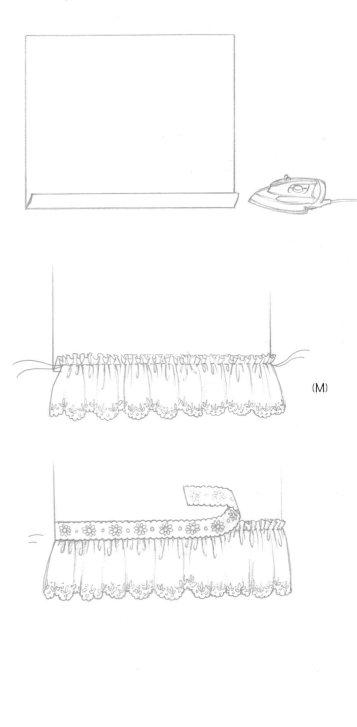

(M)

## DRESS AND FINISH GYPSY
### (continued)

**2.** With the right sides together, stitch the two unfinished edges to form a tube with the lace edging on the bottom of the tube. Repeat with the remaining piece. Turn the sleeves right-side out and gather the top edge by hand. Slip the tubes over the arms, and pull the gathers so the tops of the sleeves are snug to the shoulders. Tie off the threads. **(N)**

**3.** Make four yoyos from the blouse fabric (see page 30). With the right side of the fabric facing up, fold over a tiny hem. With a knotted, heavy thread and the #7 long darner, sew the hem with a gathering stitch. Draw the gathers together and bring the needle to the back of the yoyo through the center; pull and tie off the thread. Place a button or ribbon flower at the center of the yoyos, and stitch them to the shoulders of the doll on the blouse.

**4.** With the right sides of the vest and lining fabrics together, stitch the vest as indicated, leaving a break in the stitching. **(O)** Clip the curved sections of the seam allowance, turn the vest right-side out and press. Repeat with the ruffle fabric pieces. Close the openings by hand with the ladder stitch (page 18).

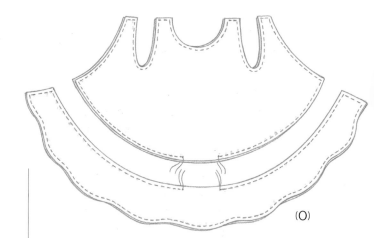

(O)

**5.** Use a zigzag stitch to join the ruffle to the vest at the bottom of the vest. Overlap the shoulder tabs from back to front and tack them in place. Sew on buttons, if desired. **(P)**

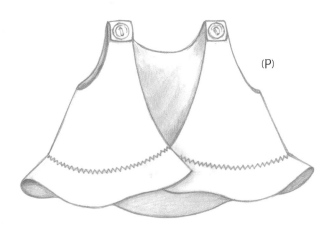

(P)

**6.** To make the overskirt, with the right sides of the fabric and the lining together, stitch the bottom edge and up to the marking on the open side. Clip the seam allowances, turn the overskirt right-side out and press. Set the overskirt aside.

**7.** To make the skirt, cut fabrics as indicated in the cutting list on page 34. Press up (with right sides together) a ¼" (6 mm) hem on one of the 45" (114.3 cm) -long edges of the ruffle. Topstitch the metallic trim over the hem edge. Gather the opposite edge to fit the 22½" (57.2 cm) skirt. Pin and stitch gathered ruffle to the bottom edge of skirt with right sides together and raw edges aligned. Press seam allowances toward skirt and topstitch seam allowances in place so they lay flat. **(Q)**

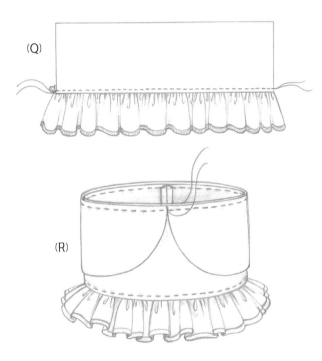

(Q)

(R)

**8.** With right sides together, stitch short edges of skirt and ruffle to make a center-back seam. Position center of overskirt at the skirt center-back seam so the shaped fronts meet in the center, as shown. Gather top edge of the skirt with ¼" (6 mm) stitches and heavy thread. Pull thread to gather the top of the skirt so it fits around the waist of the doll. Knot off threads and tack the skirt in place around the waist of the doll. **(R)**

**9.** Cover the waist with the 2" (5.1 cm) wired ribbon, and then attach a decorative jewelry finding as a buckle. Position the buckle at the front of the skirt and make a bow at the back.

**10.** Braid about twelve arm's-length pieces of 4-ply yarn and knot them at both ends with a slipknot. Also, tie a slipknot in the center of the braid. Place the center knot at the center of the forehead, wrap the braid around the head, and hand tack it in place. **(S)**

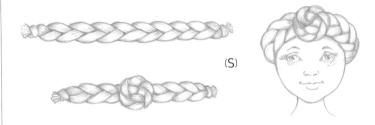

(S)

**11.** Tie an old silk scarf with tassels, a hand-kerchief, or an 11" × 8" (27.9 × 20.3 cm) remnant over her head; tack it in place. Sew beads on her head for earrings and an old necklace around her neck. **(T)**

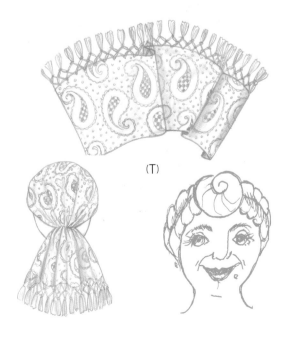

(T)

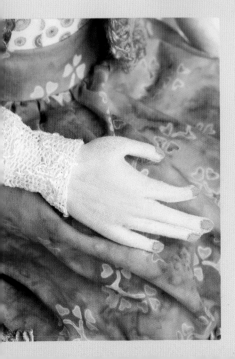

# CHAPTER 3

# Patti Medaris Culea

WHEN IT COMES TO CREATING DOLLS, ONE SIZE OR ONE concept does not, and should not, fit all. That is why I am honored to be in the same book with elinor peace bailey and Barbara Willis. Each of these wonderful ladies brings incredible creativity to life with new ideas that have no limit.

When I wrote my first doll-making book seven years ago, I simply wanted to share my love for this glorious, rewarding artistic expression with a broad range of artists. However, five books later, there was part of me that longed to bring the first-time doll maker or those with limited experience alongside me in a personal way. Reflecting back to my first years as a doll maker, I had so many questions and lacked confidence. When I read the names of great artists such as elinor and Barbara, I dreamed about how neat it would be to sit next to them, watch them work, and learn as they revealed their secrets. Now, after numerous broken needles and punctured fingers and a police blotter full of doll heads that are buried in our city's landfill, I have the privilege of collaborating with the very artists who inspired me. That's why I am thrilled to welcome you to my studio.

First a word to those who think my studio is some expansive walk-out basement that doubles as a classroom. My studio is actually a converted upstairs bedroom in San Diego that my husband, John, calls a phone booth. He knows that he enters the room at his own risk, especially barefoot. My creativity thrives in an 11' × 13' (3.7 × 4 m) phone booth. So, don't think you must have a big fancy studio to create wonderful works of art. The fact is that all you need is a sewing machine, a table, and supplies. Now that you understand we really have a lot in common, welcome to my studio.

In your hands are three books in one, and welcome to my chapter. Let's start creating that doll that you've always wanted to make.

# Getting Started

You can create two dolls using the patterns included on pages 113–116. The first doll is very simple, allowing room for all kinds of embellishments. The second doll changes a couple pattern pieces to add dimension to the body and hands, and will help you advance your doll-making skills.

## THE PATTERNS

You'll want to take a good look at all the patterns for Beth. Some have a single solid line, while others have both a solid line and a dashed line. Each represents a slightly different sewing method. You'll also see that some pattern pieces have tabs; the tabs represent the section of the seam that you leave open while sewing pieces together. The tabs help give a smooth look after you've turned the piece right side out and have to sew the opening closed.

The single solid line represents both the tracing and sewing line. It is important that you not cut the fabric on the single solid line. Instead, you will sew directly on the single solid line and therefore, you'll add seam allowance after sewing the seam. The width of the seam allowance is indicated in the instructions.

The reason for sewing seams before cutting out the pieces is to make life easier for you. Tiny areas, such the doll's fingers are especially important to sew first, and then cut out. If you cut them out before sewing, most sewing machines will "eat" the fabric. This means the fabric gets pushed down inside the throat plate and causes a mess.

Patterns with a solid line combined with a dashed line represent the pieces that can be cut out on the solid line, and then sewn together along the dashed line.

## Tracing the Patterns

There are a few ways to copy the pattern pieces. It is easiest to place the pattern pieces on a light box and trace directly onto the wrong side of the chosen fabric. Or you can make templates as on page 16.

Trace the templates or copy the pattern pieces onto the fabric with matching colored pencils. Sometimes pencil marks show through to the right side, but if you use a colored pencil that is slightly darker than the fabric, yet still visible, the markings won't show on the right side.

In the "Gallery," you'll see even more ways to be creative with these pattern pieces. Enjoy making Beth, Lydia, and your own versions of my dolls; please send me pictures!

## TIP

It is a good idea to read through the instructions before beginning the project to help you visualize the steps and prepare for them ahead of time.

# Create Beth

## MATERIALS LIST

- basic doll-making supply kit (page 14)
- specific doll-making and face painting supplies list (page 15)
- tissue paper
- double-sided bonding sheet
- cut-away stabilizer remnant
- 1/3 yard (30.5 cm) flesh-colored cotton fabric
- 18" × 22" (45.7 × 55.9 cm) printed cotton for arms and torso
- 5" (12.7 cm) length of narrow trim to cover body seam
- 18" × 22" (45.7 × 55.9 cm) striped cotton for legs
- 3–5 different 1/4 yd. (22.9 cm) printed fabrics for clothing, bolero, lining and shoes
- 1/4 yard (22.9 m) fine netting or tulle for slip
- 2 yards (1.8 m) of 1 1/2" (3.8 cm) -wide lace trim for slip
- 1/8" (3 mm) -wide elastic for slip waistband
- 4 two-hole buttons to attach legs and arms
- threads to match all fabrics
- 3 yards (2.7 m) each of various trims for the clothing
- decorative buttons for bolero and skirt
- small snaps for clothing
- good quality fiberfill
- 14 pipe cleaners for fingers and neck
- wire coat hanger
- 5 yards (4.6 m) of three different yarns for hair
- workable fixative and/or a textile medium for sealing faces
- safety pin

## CREATE THE FACE
## AND HEAD

**1.** Trace the Face onto the wrong side of a single square of flesh fabric. Notice the grainline arrow and cut the face so the arrow is parallel to the fabric selvage. Cut carefully on the traced line with straight-edged scissors.

**2.** Trace the Head Back onto the wrong side of the single layer of flesh fabric. Pin the traced head to a second piece of the same fabric with the right sides together. Sew the center-back seam (dotted line shown here), leaving a break in the stitching as indicated. Cut out the head back with a scant seam allowance at the seam, a tab at the break in the stitching, and directly on the remaining solid marked line. **(A)**

**3.** Pin the head back to the face with the right sides together. To guarantee that the pieces match, fold the face in half, match the edges, and fold a small crease at the chin and top of head. Open the face and match the creases to the seams on the head back; sew all the way around. Clip the curves and turn the face and head back right side out through the opening. Fill the head firmly with stuffing (page 17). **(B)**

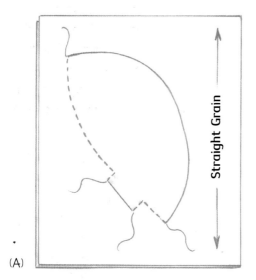

(A)

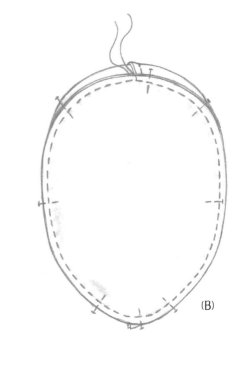

(B)

**···· TIP**

Wrinkles along the seamline means there isn't enough stuffing inside. It's amazing how much stuffing can be placed into such a small item. Keep pushing the stuffing in until the wrinkles disappear.

# CREATE THE TORSO AND LEGS

**1.** Cut a piece of flesh-colored fabric 4½" × 11" (11.4 × 27.9 cm) and a piece of the print torso fabric 7" × 11" (17.8 × 27.9 cm). Sew the two pieces together along one long side with right sides facing. Press the seam open.

**2.** Trace the Body Front onto the wrong side of the pieced fabric, positioning the line on the pattern piece directly over the seam. Cut out one body front along the solid line. Fold the remaining fabric in half with right sides together and with the seam aligned, and trace the Body Back with the line on the pattern piece directly over the seam. **(C)**

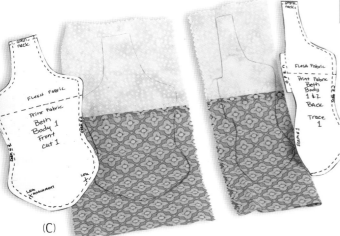

(C)

**3.** Sew the center-back seam (indicated on the pattern) directly on the solid line, leaving a break in the stitching at the tab, and backstitching at the top of the neck. Cut out the body back with a scant seam allowance at the seam, around the tab and along the remaining solid marked line. Press the seam open. **(D)**

**···· TIP**

I find it helpful to slip a pipe cleaner inside the neck opening to give the neck more stability. Using a hemostat, slide the pipe cleaner down along the back seam of the body back. Continue to add stuffing around the pipe cleaner.

**4.** Pin and stitch narrow trim to the right side of the body front to cover the seam. Pin the body front to the body back with right sides together. Machine sew from the neck opening all the way around to the other side of the neck opening, easing the stitching around the curves and leaving the neck unstitched; backstitch at the neck opening. Turn the body right-side out through the opening and fill it firmly with stuffing. When the stuffing starts popping out of the back opening, ladder stitch it closed, and finish filling the body through the neck opening. **(E)**

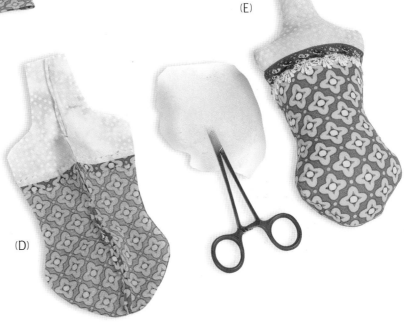

(E)

(D)

## CREATE THE TORSO
## AND LEGS (continued)

**5.** For the legs, sew two pieces of fabric together as you did for the body; a 9½" × 16" (24.1 × 40.6 cm) piece of striped fabric for the upper leg and a 5" × 16" (12.7 × 40.6 cm) flesh-colored piece for the foot. Trace two Legs onto the wrong side of the fabric so that the dashed line on the pattern is positioned over the seam. Double the fabric and with the right sides together, sew all the way around both legs. Cut out the legs with ¼" (6 mm) seam allowance. Place them on the table with the toes facing each other and cut a slit near the top of each leg as marked on the pattern piece. By placing the toes facing each other you'll guarantee that you have a right and a left leg. **(F)**

**6.** Turn the legs right-side out by pulling them through the openings. Stuff them firmly up to the knee. With the knees facing out, machine sew across both legs. Finish filling the rest of the legs lightly with stuffing. Ladder stitch the slit closed at the top of each leg. Hand stitch trim to legs to cover seams.

**7.** To attach the legs to the body, thread a long needle with strong thread and knot the ends together. Attach the thread to one side of the body at the marking, and then push the needle through the leg slightly above the slit and pick up a button. Go through both button holes and back into the leg and through the body to the other side. Do the same with the remaining leg. Go back and forth through the legs and body and catching the buttons at least three times. Anchor off the thread inside the body under the leg. **(G)**

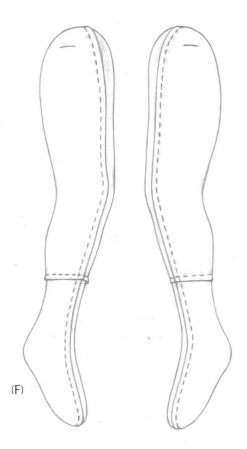

(F)

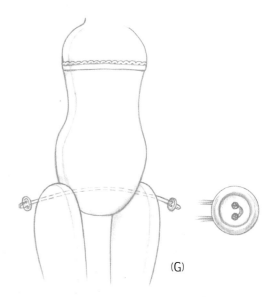

(G)

## •••• TIP

Use buttons with just two holes to attach the legs; four-hole buttons don't allow the legs to move freely.

# CREATE THE ARMS AND HANDS

**1.** Trace two Arms and two Hands onto the wrong side of the chosen fabric. Double the fabric so the right sides are together and machine sew directly on the traced lines, leaving the arms and hands open as indicated on the pattern. Cut around the stitching with straight-edge scissors leaving a ¼" (6 mm) seam allowance; clip the curves.

**2.** Turn the arms right-side out and fill them with stuffing to within 1" (2.5 cm) from the opening. Turn the hands right-side out, and draw lines for the fingers. Refer to the pattern and machine stitch the fingers starting near the palm, and then sew to the tip of the first finger. Swivel the hand and machine sew back down to the palm. Do this with each finger, leaving long thread tails. (H)

(H)

**3.** To bury the thread tails inside the hands, thread a needle with the two existing threads on each side of the fingers. Carefully push the needle inside the hand, and come out at the wrist opening taking care not to catch any of the hand fabric. Remove the threads from the needle and tie a double knot, pulling the knot tightly against the inside of the finger. Cut the threads. Repeat for each finger and with each side. (I)

(I)

**4.** Bend back both ends of six pipe cleaners, and then bend four pipe cleaners in half. Insert one of the folded pipe cleaners so one end goes in the first finger and the other end goes in the next finger. Repeat for the two remaining fingers and the other hand. Insert a straight pipe cleaner in one of the thumbs, and then wrap it around the centerfold of the other two pipe cleaners. Leave about 2½" (6.4 cm) of the straight pipe cleaner sticking out of the hand. Repeat for the other hand. (J)

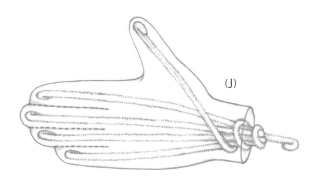

(J)

**5.** Fill the palms with minimal stuffing. As you do this, be sure you create a left and right hand. The stuffing pushes the pipe cleaners against the back of the hands creating the look of bones. Insert the hands into the lower arm openings and slide the straight pipe cleaner up into the arms. Finish stuffing the lower arm and wrist.

**6.** Whipstitch the hands to the arms. Cover the seams with more trim by hand stitching.

## ATTACH THE HEAD AND CREATE THE FACE

**1.** To attach the head, pinch the neck closed with the hemostats and rock the head onto the neck. Pin the head in place and ladder stitch it to the neck.

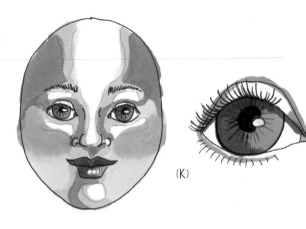

(K)

**···TIP**

You can attach the head before or after drawing and coloring the face. I generally attach the head first so I have something to hold on to while I work on the face. Others prefer not to in case they don't like the face and want to sew another head.

**2.** Trace the facial features from the Face pattern (page 114) onto a piece of tissue paper. Place the tissue paper over the doll's face. With a pencil and pressing hard, trace over the features. This will tear the tissue paper slightly, transferring the features onto the fabric.

**3.** Remove the tissue paper and outline the features with a brown permanent pen. Refer to the drawing above and use a brown colored pencil for the shaded areas of the face. Add highlights with a white pencil and blush the cheeks with a red or rose-colored pencil.

**···TIP**

Another way to transfer features is to draw them on cheesecloth. Because cheesecloth is loosely woven, the pencil marks go through to the head.

**4.** Choose three colored pencils for the eyes: a light, medium, and dark. Fill in the irises with the lightest color (Patti used Celadon Green, Peacock Blue, and Mulberry). Over the lightest color, use the medium color to shade underneath the upper eyelid and down one side of the iris and all the way to the pupil. Apply the darkest color on top of the medium color under the upper eyelid and just slightly along the outer edge of the iris. **(K)**

# Create the Clothes and Finish Beth

**5.** Choose a medium and dark-colored pencil to color the lips (Patti used Carmine Red and Crimson Red). Fill in both the upper and lower lip with the medium color. Since the upper lip is generally curved inward use the darker color to darken and shade this lip. Extend the darker color a little bit to one side of the lower lip that would be more shaded, like the eyes.

## •••• TIP

At this point I usually spray the face with workable fixative. There are several good ones on the market. Krylon and Prismacolor are easy to find at your local craft and/or art store.

**6.** Finish the face by highlighting it with permanent pens and gel pens. Blacken the pupils with a black pen. Outline the irises with a darker colored pen. Draw the rods that radiate out from the pupils with the same pen. With a brown pen, draw the eyelashes and eyebrows. Go over the eyelids, nostrils, and flare of the nose with the brown pen. With a red pen, outline the lips and draw the creases in the upper and lower lip. With the white gel pen whiten the whites of the eyes and add a highlight on the light side of the pupil. Smear a little of the white gel from the pen on the lower lip.

**7.** Seal the face with either the fixative used previously or a textile medium.

## CREATE THE SLIP AND SKIRT

**1.** For the slip, cut the tulle 8" × 20" (20.3 × 50.8 cm). Machine sew the 1½" (3.8 cm) -wide lace trim along the bottom edge. Sew the short edges with the right sides together to create a center-back seam and form a circle of fabric. Fold the top edge ½" (1.3 cm) to the wrong side and sew along the cut edge to form a casing for the elastic; leave an opening in the stitching. Measure the waist and cut the elastic to fit. Insert elastic into the casing through the opening, and hand-sew the opening closed.

**2.** Cut the upper skirt fabric 7" × 20" (17.8 × 50.8 cm). Cut the lower skirt fabric 4" × 20" (10.2 × 50.8 cm). With the right sides together, machine stitch the bottom fabric to the skirt fabric. Stitch trim over the seam on the right side of the fabric. **(L)**

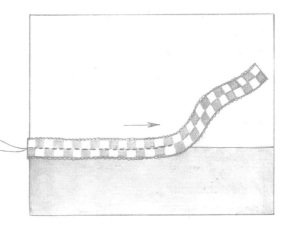

(L)

## CREATE THE SLIP
## AND SKIRT (continued)

**3.** Sew a row of machine gathering stitches along the top of the skirt. Finish the short sides of the skirt for about 1½" (3.8 cm) from the top edge by folding over the cut edge to the wrong side ¼" (6 mm), press and stitch (for reference see the illustration for step 5).

**4.** Cut the waistband fabric 2½" × 7" (6.4 × 17.8 cm). Press the long edges ¼" (6 mm) to the wrong side, and then finger press the waistband in half. Unfold the waistband and with the right sides together, gather and pin the skirt to one long edge of the waistband so the waistband extends ¼" (6 mm) on one end and 1½" (3.8 cm) on the opposite end, as shown. Machine stitch, making sure the gathers are straight and evenly distributed. Be careful, it's easy to catch a gather at an angle and create a crinkle, rather than a gather.

**5.** Refold the waistband in half lengthwise with the right sides together. Machine stitch the ends and trim the corners as shown. Turn the waistband right-side out and press. The waistband will extend slightly on one side. (M)

**6.** Slipstitch the pressed edge of the waist-band over the seam on the inside of the skirt. (N)

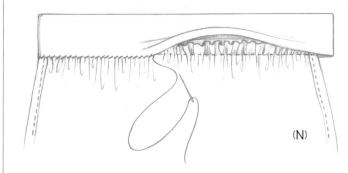

(N)

**7.** Sew the back seam with the right sides together, stopping at the bottom of the finished opening created in step 3. Fold the bottom fabric, wrong sides together, and press flat. From the right side, machine stitch directly over the previous stitching, through the trim, to secure the hem of the lower skirt.

**8.** Hand sew a small snap to the inside of the waistband and a decorative button on the right side. Sew more decorative buttons along the trim on the skirt as desired.

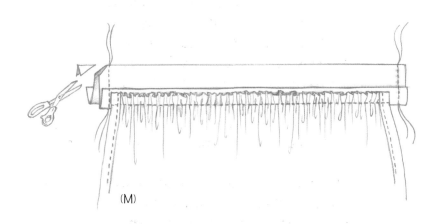

(M)

## CREATE THE BOLERO

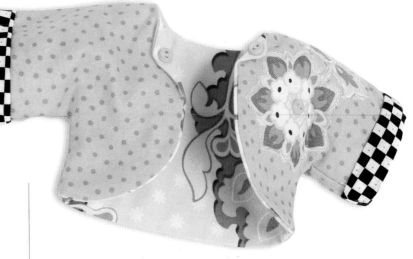

**1.** Trace the Bolero pattern onto both the outside and lining fabric and cut them out.

**2.** Choose a motif from the print fabric for an appliqué to decorate the bolero. Press a double-sided bonding sheet to the wrong side of the print fabric, and cut out the design. Remove the backing paper and fuse the design to the right side of the bolero fabric. Pin a piece of cut-away stabilizer slightly larger than the appliqué to the wrong side of the bolero under the appliqué. Machine sew a straight stitch around the appliqué catching the stabilizer in the stitching.

**3.** Cut two strips of fabric 1½" × 5¾" (3.8 × 14.6 cm) for the sleeve hem bands (black and white checked fabric was used). Machine stitch the bands to the end of the sleeves on the lining fabric with the right sides together.

**4.** With the right sides together, pin the underarm seams of the outside fabric and stitch from the ends of the sleeves to the lower hem edge. Repeat with the lining fabric. (O)

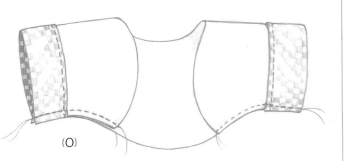

(O)

---

•••• **TIP**

When you want to decorate your doll's clothing, look to your printed fabrics. Many times isolating a motif from the fabric can serve as an appliqué.

**5.** Turn the lining right-side out and pin it to the outside fabric with the right sides together along the neck and bottom edges. Stitch, easing around the curves. Don't stitch the sleeve openings; the bands will extend beyond the lining sleeves.

**6.** Turn the bolero right-side out by reaching inside one sleeve with a pair of hemostats. Grab the other sleeve with the hemostats and pull the entire jacket carefully through the opening. You'll need to adjust the sleeves so the lining and outside fabric fit together smoothly. Use an iron to press all the seams smooth and to press the black and white bands to the inside so that about ½" (1.3 cm) shows on the right side. Ladder stitch the bands to the inside of the sleeves.

**7.** On the front, press the top corners back toward the shoulders to form lapels and hand sew a button on each to hold them in place.

## CREATE THE SHOES

**1.** Fold the outside shoe fabric and shoe lining fabric in half with right sides together. Trace the Shoe template two times onto the wrong side of the outside fabric and the lining fabric and cut out the Shoes on the marked line.

**2.** With the right-sides together, machine stitch from the top of the heel, down the heel, across the bottom of the shoe (leave a break in the stitching along the bottom for turning the shoes right-side out), and then up the front to the shoe opening. Leave the shoe opening unstitched. Repeat with the remaining shoe pieces and the lining pieces.

**3.** Turn the lining right-side out. Pin the shoe and lining with right sides together and seams aligned. Machine stitch around the shoe opening. Turn the shoe right-side out by reaching through the opening in the lining with a pair of hemostats and grabbing the toe of the shoe. Pull both the outside fabric and lining through the opening. With the hemostats, push the lining toe to the inside of the shoe toe. Ladder stitch the opening closed. Finger-press the edge and the shoe is ready for embellishment. (P)

**4.** Cut the bow fabric into two 3¹/₄" × 1¹/₄" (8.2 × 3.1 cm) pieces. Fold each piece with the right sides together, and machine stitch the three open sides, leaving an opening at the center. Turn each piece through the opening and hand sew the opening closed. Run gathering stitches across the center and pull the thread to gather up each strip. Hand sew a button at the center of each and attach them to the top of each shoe. Slip the shoes on the doll and tack them in place to secure them. (Q)

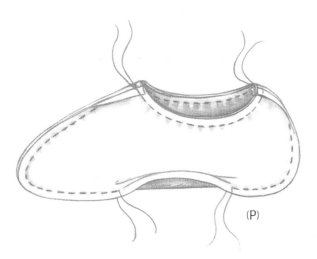

(P)

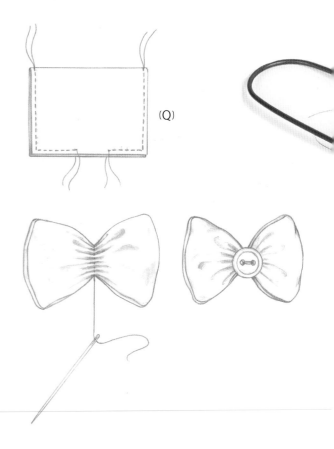

(Q)

## CREATE THE HAIR

**1.** Bend a coat hanger in half so the wires are 3" (7.6 cm) apart. Wrap the three yarns you've chosen for hair around the wires to create a 14" (35.6 cm) length of wrapped yarn. It helps to have something at the end to keep the two wires separated. **(R)**

**2.** With your sewing machine, sew down the center of the wrapped yarn with either a zigzag or a straight stitch. Slip the stitched yarn off the wires and pin it to the doll's head, starting at the back and wrapping it along the face seam. Tack the hair to the head in several places, and tack or glue a small bow in her hair.

(S)

## PUTTING BETH TOGETHER

**1.** To attach the arms at the shoulders, thread a hand-sewing needle with strong thread and knot it. Attach the thread to the shoulder, and then push the needle into the arm toward the top. Run the needle through to the outside and pick up a button. Go through both button holes and back through the arm and into the shoulder. Go back through the arm and button once more and anchor the thread back at the shoulder. Do the same with the other arm. **(S)**

**2.** Place the skirt and bolero on Beth and she is ready to sit quietly on a shelf or chair. By now she's pretty tired and needs a rest.

(R)

# Making Lydia

Just a few changes to the basic body pattern and a different set of clothes will create a very different doll. Adding seams to the body front, a few separate fingers and a different foot will change the doll body and give it more shape without adding too much work. And, of course, different clothes with lots of trims give every doll their own unique appeal.

Read through the instructions carefully before you begin because you will often be referred back to the step-by-step instructions for Beth. The biggest differences between Beth and Lydia are in the shaping and seaming of the torso, legs and hands.

## MATERIALS LIST

- basic doll-making supply kit (page 14)
- specific doll-making and face-painting supplies list (page 15)
- tissue paper
- ⅓ yard (30.5 cm) flesh-colored cotton fabric
- 18" × 22" (45.7 × 55.9 cm) printed cotton for body
- 18" × 22" (45.7 × 55.9 cm) striped cotton for legs
- 3 different ¼ yd. (22.9 cm) fabrics for clothing, shoes, bows, baubles
- ¼ yard (22.9 cm) stretchy lace for wrist warmers
- variety of lace edgings and trims
- 4 two-hole buttons to attach legs and arms
- thread to match all fabrics
- narrow ribbon for elbows and knees
- good quality fiberfill
- 14 pipe cleaners for fingers and neck
- workable fixative and/or a textile medium for sealing faces
- small piece of Tibetan Goat hair for hair
- 1 yard (91.4 cm) of 2½" (6.4 cm) -wide lace trim for skirt
- 1 yard (91.4 cm) of 1" (2.5 cm) -wide lace trim for skirt
- old sweater to cut up for bolero
- yarn to match sweater
- tapestry needle for yarn
- ¼ yard (22.9 cm) cotton eyelet fabric for slip
- 2 yards (1.6 m) of 1½" (3.8 cm) -wide lace trim for slip
- ⅛" (3 cm) -wide elastic for waistband
- small snaps and decorative button for waistband
- decorative buttons for bolero and shoes
- seed beads and drop beads for baubles
- size 11 needle for beading

# CREATE THE DOLL BODY

**1.** You can use the same face template used for Beth (page 114), or use the template below. Follow steps 1–3 on page 48 to make the head. Set it aside. **(A)**

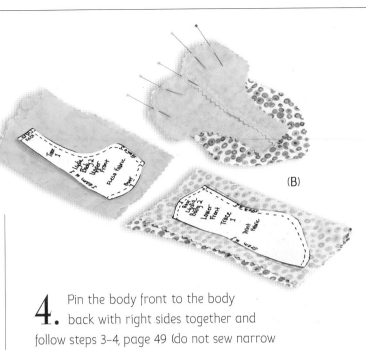

(B)

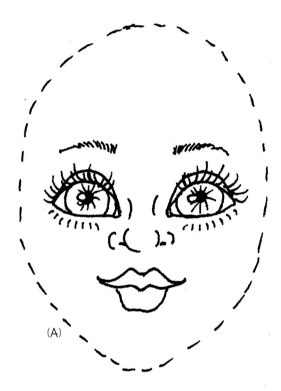

(A)

**2.** For the body back follow step 1 and step 3 on page 49.

**3.** With the fabrics folded with right sides together, trace the Lydia Body Upper Front onto flesh-colored fabric and the Lydia Body Lower Front onto print fabric. Before cutting out these pieces, stitch the center-front seam on both. Cut out the pieces with a scant seam allowance at the seams and directly on the traced lines. Press the seams open. Pin the upper body to the lower body with the right sides together and stitch.

**4.** Pin the body front to the body back with right sides together and follow steps 3–4, page 49 (do not sew narrow trim over the seam until later). **(B)**

**5.** Before cutting the fabric for Lydia's leg and foot, place the Foot pattern on the Leg pattern so the dashed lines are together and tape the Foot in place. Trace the entire leg and foot as one and then trace the new Leg/Foot onto card stock (page 16) to make the template. Piece the leg fabric as in step 5 on page 50. Fold the leg fabric in half with right sides together and trace the Leg/Foot template twice. Follow steps 5–7 on page 50 to make, stuff, and attach the legs to the body, except the foot. After cutting out the leg, fold the toe of the foot so the seams match and sew across the curve of the toes. Instead of sewing across the knees, tie a pretty ribbon around each knee. **(C)**

(C)

## CREATE THE DOLL BODY
**(continued)**

**6.** Trace and sew the arms and hands, referring to the instructions for Beth, step 1 on page 51. Make sure you use the Hand template marked Lydia, the Arm template is the same for both dolls. Stitch the hands slowly and carefully as they have separate fingers. Clip between each finger and the curves at the wrist. Turn the hands right-side out using hemostats or turning tubes, but turn each finger separately before turning the entire hand. (D)

**7.** Using a brown-colored pencil, draw a line between the two connected fingers. The colored line creates shading and gives you a good reference for sewing. Machine stitch on the line, leaving long thread tails at the beginning. Refer to step 3, page 51 to bury the thread tails inside the hands. Follow steps 4–5, page 51 to add wire and stuff the hands.

**8.** Stitch and turn the arms right-side out and fill them with stuffing to the elbows. As for the legs, tie a ribbon around the arms at the elbows then lightly fill the arms to the wrists.

**9.** Insert the hands into the lower arm openings and slide the straight pipe cleaner up into the arms. Finish stuffing the lower arm and wrist. Whipstitch the hands to the arms, and then the arms to the torso as for Beth (page 57).

**10.** Outline Lydia's fingernails with a brown pen; then color them with a colored pencil. Cut two 2" (5.1 cm) squares of stretchy lace. Fold each square in half with right sides facing, and then sew one seam to create tubes. Turn the tubes right-side out. Slip the tubes on the wrists and tuck under the raw edges to create fancy wrist warmers. (E)

(E)

**11.** Follow steps 1–7, pages 52–53 to attach the head to the body and color in the face. You can copy and refer to Beth's face or you can use the template on page 114. The hair will be attached after Lydia is dressed.

**12.** Hand sew lace and trim to cover the seams on the torso front and back. (For Beth this was done by machine, but on Lydia it has to be done by hand.)

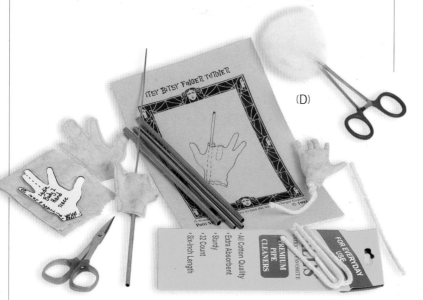

(D)

# Create the Clothes and Finish Lydia

## CREATE THE CLOTHING

**1.** Make the slip as in step 1, page 53. Lydia's skirt has a hem ruffle as a design variation. Cut the skirt fabric 7" × 20" (17.8 × 50.8 cm) for the upper skirt and 4" × 36" (10.2 × 91.4 cm) for the ruffle. Fold the ruffle piece in half lengthwise with the wrong sides together. Cut a 36" (91.4 cm) length of 2½" (6.4 cm) -wide lace trim. Pin the lace to the wrong side of the ruffle along the ruffle raw edges. The lace will peak out from under the ruffle when the skirt is complete to look like a petticoat.

**2.** Machine baste the ruffle top edges together, catching the lace in the stitching. Sew a row of gathering stitches next to the basting stitches. Pull the gathering threads so the ruffle fits the lower edge of the skirt. Pin the ruffle and skirt with the right sides together; stitch.

**3.** Cut a length of trim and 1" (2.5 cm) -wide lace to fit along the top edge of the ruffle and topstitch both to the skirt, just above the ruffle. Fold the skirt with the right sides together, and machine sew the seam to within 1½" (3.8 cm) from the top. Sew and attach the waistband, following steps 3–8, page 54.

**4.** For the Bolero, trace the template on an old sweater and cut it out (there is no lining for this bolero). Set your sewing machine for a narrow zigzag stitch and stitch around all the raw edges to prevent the sweater from unraveling. **(F)**

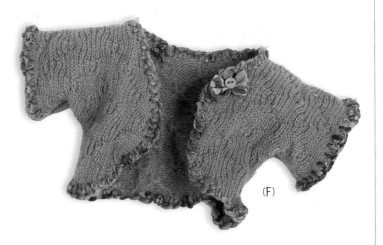

(F)

**5.** With the right sides together, pin and machine stitch the underarm seams as in step 4, page 55. Finish the raw edges with yarn and a blanket stitch (page 18).

**6.** Make a fabric bow as for Beth's shoes (step 4, page 56) and hand sew it to the bolero lapel.

## CREATE THE SHOES

**1.** Fold the outside shoe fabric and the lining fabric in half with right sides together. Trace the Shoe Top template two times and the Shoe Sole one time on the outside fabric. Trace the Shoe Top two times on the lining fabric as well. Cut out all the pieces along the traced lines.

**2.** With the right sides together, sew the front and heel seams of the outside and lining fabrics for both shoes. Turn the lining pieces right-side out and pin them to the shoe tops with the right sides together. **(G)**

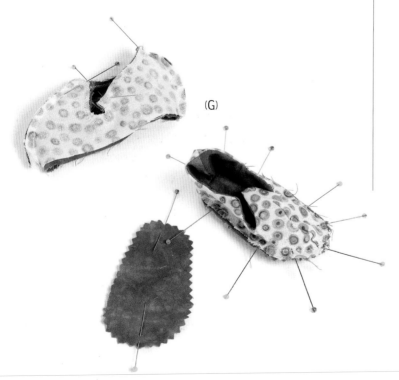

(G)

**3.** Machine stitch the shoe top to the lining along the shoe opening, finger-press the seam. Turn the shoes so that the lining is on the outside with the main fabric inside.

**4.** Fold a shoe sole in half lengthwise and finger-crease the fold. Pin the shoe sole to the shoe top matching the creases in the sole to the seams in the top. Machine stitch all the way around, starting and ending at the heel. Trim the seams with pinking shears and clip the curves. Repeat for the remaining shoe. Turn the shoes right-side out. Make two more fabric bows as in step 4, page 56, and hand sew a bow in the center of each shoe top. Slip the shoes on Lydia.

## CREATE THE BAUBLES

**1.** Make eight baubles to dangle from the ribbons at the elbows and knees. Trace the Bauble template eight times on the chosen fabric. Thread a size 11 needle with strong thread that matches the fabric; knot the single long end. Hand sew a gathering stitch along the outer edge of a circle. Pull the gathers slightly; then place a small amount of stuffing inside. Continue to pull the gathers tightly to create a fabric ball. Before anchoring the gathering threads, poke the end of one of the ribbons (already tied to the doll's elbows and knees) inside the bauble. Stitch through the ribbon and then around the top of the bauble; do not cut the thread. **(H)**

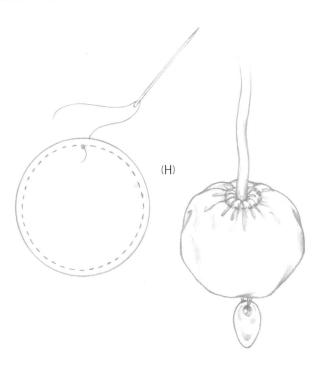

(H)

**2.** To add beads to the bottom of the baubles, weave the needle down to the bottom center of the bauble and pick up a drop bead on the needle. Weave the needle back up to the top, knot the threads and bury them in the bauble. Repeat to make and attach seven more baubles to the remaining ribbon ends

**2.** Score the hide part of the fur with scissors to make a piece 3¹/₂" × 5" (8.9 × 12.7 cm). Tear, don't cut, along the scores. If you cut the fur, you'll lose a lot of hair. To create the flaps for adjusting the fur to the doll's head from each side, you'll need to score in two places. Starting at the lower edge, score and tear two times, 1¹/₄" (3.1 cm) long and 1¹/₄" (3.1 cm) from each side as shown in the photograph. Again, tear after scoring, being careful not to tear too far.  (I)

(I)

## FINISH THE DOLL

**1.** To attach the arms at the shoulders, thread a hand-sewing needle with strong thread and knot it. Attach the thread to the shoulder, and then push the needle through the arm toward the top and pick up a button. Go through both holes of the button, back through the arm and into the shoulder. Go back through the arm and button once more, and then anchor the thread at the shoulder. Do the same with the other arm. Slip the skirt and bolero on your doll.

**3.** Pin the fur to the top of the head along the seam, with the fur side against her face. With a needle and strong thread, hand sew the fur along the seam from one side of her face to the other. Flip the hair back away from her face, fold under the two sides and hand sew them to the head. Fold down the middle piece and hand sew to the head. Make another fabric bow and tack in her hair, and Lydia is finished.

# CHAPTER 4

# Barbara Willis

Keeping it simple is our goal for this book, but making it interesting is my focus here, and I am so glad you are ready to open yourself up to play dolls!

I am delighted to be collaborating with two of my favorite friends and cloth-doll artists, elinor peace bailey and Patti Culea. Our passion for the doll as an art form drew us together many years ago. Our mutual admiration for each other's artistic path has helped us form a strong bond of friendship, as well as a friendly competition to become better selves and artists. The diversity of our approaches to doll making has worked as inspiration as we have carved out our own signature styles. So although each of us has our own color sensibility and artistic strengths, we are able to work side by side and bask in the success of the creative process that we each follow.

As a mentor and friend, elinor has long been urging me on. Her creative freedom helps me look beyond myself and want to reach further. Her color sense and artistic ability, with nothing more than a box of colored pencils, makes me want to stand up and cheer. The job of being my mentor weighs heavy and she always rises to the occasion with her friendship, willingness to listen, and her words of wisdom.

Patti has shared her soul with the doll world and has touched us all. Her books on cloth-doll making have inspired many, and they have become essential for cloth-doll makers. Beading, painting, and silk dying are just a few of the tricks she pulls out of her hat for her unique creations. Patti has lavished her artistic talents on her beautiful cloth dolls and shares it with all of us.

We have titled this book *Cloth Doll Workshop* because it starts at the beginning with basic construction techniques and takes you along side us in step-by-step fashion as we create our version of these dolls. Since the concept of this book is to offer you a beginner cloth-doll workshop, I asked myself what exactly a beginner doll is, and realized that the answer is the doll that you choose to begin with—so let's begin. Use these pages as the springboard for your own creative process, allowing you to push beyond what you find here as you develop your own doll style.

Dolls touch us in so many ways; they are an extension of the human form, a creative outlet, and a sharing of ourselves with others. A basic cloth doll can be a play doll meant for a child or it can be a simple creative outlet in cloth-doll form. My dolls seem to fall in the later category, more as a creative outlet for the inner artist. Although I made several dolls for my children, I learned that I loved the doll-making process the most.

You will find differences in style between elinor, Patti, and myself, as well as in the requirements for each doll. We all have our favorite supplies and techniques. You'll find what works best for you. Experiment with all the projects we are sharing with you, and find the approach that gives you the most rewarding experience as you build your own personal toolbox and create your own personalized cloth doll.

As I present my basic cloth doll techniques—including construction, several costume ideas, and full facial development and coloration—keep in mind that the treasure hunt for ideas and materials is as much fun as the designing. Building a worthy stash of fabrics, notions, and trims to pull from is a delightful part of cloth doll making. If you are wondering if your doll will have the right trims, the answer is yes—because you pick what you like—the colors, textures, and styles that draw you in. Local craft stores, scrapbook stores, and fabric shops have heaps of stuff just waiting to go home with you. If you love vintage, then flea markets, garage sales, and thrift stores should be the focus of your gathering. As you can probably tell from my dolls, I love vintage textiles, and I lavish my dolls with items from my stash.

It is important to have a space in which you can create and let your imagination have its way—a space that inspires you to want to make art, a spot you can call your own. It does not have to be a big space; even a table that isn't earmarked for the evening meal is a start.

I have long had a large space in which to work, but for just as long I've needed a professional organizer to dig in and straighten it out! I seem to accumulate more things than I have space for and have a larger than normal appetite for vintage findings, trims, ribbons, decorative papers, rubber stamps, beads, charms, and buttons. Many of the fabrics I am currently using are fabrics I purchased long ago—I have kept them so long that I think they have become vintage! However, from all my fabric and trims, which are readily available and always close at hand, comes inspiration and an environment for creativity, and for that I am grateful. I don't have much wall space, so I have piles of things that I love all around me, with little vignettes of special collections within eyeshot to keep me happy. Within the messy veneer lies a studio ready to encourage the next design or project.

When I am starting a project, I pull from my stash more fabrics and embellishments than I will use, but the mountain of color, fiber, texture, and glitz gets me jump-started without hesitation. I consider the mountain of stuff the casting call or audition, while the finished project is the final result of the sorting, incorporating, and eliminating.

First, you'll want to choose the main costume fabric, which will lead you to your ribbon choices, button selections, and embellishment options. So spread out all your selections, and enjoy the emotion and feeling they provide, and then get ready to play dolls!

# Getting Started

This trio of dolls is made from one pattern, but as you can see the design elements can be adapted with one or two simple changes to make different dolls. Remember, my first lesson in doll designing—there are really no mistakes; it's just a little bit of fabric. Try again and have fun in the process. Embrace the learning curve and enjoy all that it teaches you.

## THE PATTERNS

The basic doll pattern was built around a doll I fittingly named My Marie. My Marie is a lovely rendition of an earlier era with a wide skirt made of French toile fabric. But, if the skirt is narrowed at the hips and hem, you create a totally different look, such as a casual lounge outfit reminiscent of Holly Golightly from *Breakfast at Tiffany's* fame, and so this doll is appropriately named Holly. A more

drastic narrowing of the lower hem edge of the lower pattern piece transforms this design (with a little bit of stuffing and a velvet tail) into Shy, a lovely mermaid.

The basic pattern includes two Arm/Hand options, one with a thumb and one without. The thumb is small and a bit fussy to sew, so you can choose to make the hand with or without the thumb—both are lovely and delicate—simply choose the option that is right for you.

Copy all the pattern pieces for the doll you intend to make and the feature placement guide on page 119 onto card stock paper at your copy center. Cut the patterns out carefully on the line to create pattern templates as explained on page 16. Careful template cutting is essential to a good transfer. Punch holes in the feature template guide with a 1/8" (3 mm) punch as indicated on the guide.

Holly

My Marie

Shy

# CREATING A
# BEAUTIFUL FACE

The face always seems to be the biggest challenge for many new, as well as seasoned, cloth doll makers. There are two different methods for creating the dolls faces explained below. The first method uses one of the three transfers provided, while the second method teaches you how to draw your own face with detailed drawing instructions. Feel free to mix and match the faces with the dolls.

## Full-Color Face Transfers

There are three full-color face transfers in the pattern section of this book (see page 117). This option requires a fabric inkjet transfer sheet that is copied on an inkjet printer. Buy good quality transfer sheets because they are made from high-thread-count fabric and are colorfast. They usually come in packages of three and are readily available at fabric and craft stores.

**1.** Insert a fabric sheet into the paper feed of an inkjet printer and copy the full-colored faces on page 117.

**2.** Heat set the copy according to the manufacturer's instructions on the fabric sheet packaging.

**3.** Position the Feature Placement template over the facial features, matching the eyeholes over the pupils.

**4.** Trace around the entire template shape with a purple fade-away marker. The ink will bleed through to the other side. Trim just outside the outline marking.

**5.** Continue to the section "Make and Attach the Head," (pages 79–80).

My Marie

Holly

Shy

## Drawing Facial Features

If you prefer to draw your own face, use the Feature Placement template to help you develop your own facial-features style. Feature placement and size (relative to each other) is the key to a good cloth doll face. If the eyes are too big you can't balance the face by giving her a small nose; all the features need to work together as a balanced unit. All of this is explained in the step-by-step photos and instructions. Feel free to choose any face for any of the dolls. Keep a copy of the color-face transfer nearby as reference for feature size, placement, and coloration as you create your own features.

Start with a single layer of flesh-colored fabric and a selection of permanent color pens with tips no larger than 01. Sakura Micron Pigma pens come as small as 05 and are great for small faces and details. Don't confuse an 005 tip, which is much too large for this scale doll with an 05 tip, which is acceptable.

## •••• TIP

Begin by drawing the features on the side of the face that is most difficult for you. If you do your best work on your easier side first, it's hard to duplicate your work on the side you have less control over. You can also try turning the face upside down to create curves and strokes on the side that is harder for you. These tips will help keep the facial features balanced and look similar.

My Marie

Holly

Shy

## CREATING A BEAUTIFUL FACE
(continued)

**1.** Lay the Feature Placement template over a piece of flesh-colored fabric and use it to mark the eyes, nose, mouth dots, and face outlines. Use a mechanical pencil to mark the pupil holes. Trace the nose and mouth dots and the complete outline of the feature template with purple fade-away marker, letting the ink bleed through to the other side of the fabric. Position a small ruler or other straight edge over the mouth dot and across the face from side to side. Draw a line across the face with the purple fade-away marker. Draw another line across the nose dot with the fade-away marker. (**A**)

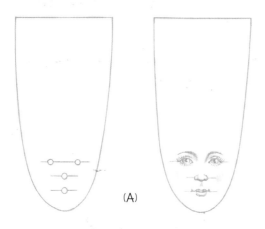

(A)

**2.** *Holly and My Marie's Eyes.* Look at the full-color face transfer for size and shape reference. For detailed instructions for drawing Shy's downcast eyes, see page 89. Use a black Pigma pen (01 tip) to create the pupil by filling in the eyehole dot. Use a pastel gel pen or colored pencil to draw a small circle around the pupil to create the iris. Outline the iris carefully with brown Pigma pen, keeping the shape round. Use the mechanical pencil to draw a football shape around each iris to create the outer eye line. Make sure the football shape touches the top and bottom of the iris. Go over the pencil lines with a black Pigma pen.

**3.** Finish the eyes, referring to the picture. Use a black Pigma pen to add the lashes so they come off the eye line in light wispy strokes. Study the direction of the lashes, as it is different for each eye. Use dots and a white gel pen to fill in the whites of the eyes (this may take two or three applications; let ink dry completely between applications). Also, add a highlight in each eye at the two-o'clock position in each iris.

**4.** *The Eyebrows.* Create the eyebrows. Dot in the arch and shape of each eyebrow with a fade-away marker. Once you are happy with the placement, then stroke in the brow lines over the dots with a brown or black Pigma pen.

My Marie

**5.** Choose from two mouth variations, and draw the shape with a brown Pigma pen. For My Marie's mouth, draw a double-loop bow to create the upper lip and a U-shape to create the bottom lip. Add the line that divides the mouth, which is a curved smile with wings. Color in the lips with colored pencils. Use a darker shade on the top lip and a lighter shade on the bottom lip.

For the Holly/Shy mouth, draw a lazy M-shape across the purple fade-away line that spans the mouth dot to form the middle of the mouth. Draw another lazy M-shape above to create the upper lip outline. Draw a lazy U-shape below the middle line to create the lower lip. Color the lips with colored pencils; use a darker shade on the top lip and a lighter shade on the bottom lip.

**6.** Draw the nose with the brown Pigma pen. Notice that My Marie and Shy only have nostril dots, while Holly has a more defined nose shape. Choose the nose you want to use and lightly draw in the detail. If you want, you can draw the nose first with a mechanical pencil.

**7.** To finish the face apply powdered blush to the cheeks with a sponge applicator. Apply two to three colors of eye shadow with a short liner brush (Barbara likes to use two to three colors). When the face is complete, apply a spray fixative to seal the color on the face. Spray outdoors and let the fixative dry completely.

**8.** Continue to "Make and Attach the Head," (pages 79–80).

Holly

Shy

## ····● TIP

I often use the tip of a hand-sewing needle and white acrylic paint to make a dot.

# Make My Marie

It is a good idea to read through the instructions before beginning to help you visualize the steps and prepare for them ahead of time. Attach the open toe presser foot and set your machine to a stitch length of 1.5 (page 17).

## MATERIALS LIST

- basic doll-making supply kit (page 14)
- specific doll-making and face-painting supplies list (page 15)
- tissue paper
- ¼ yard (22.9 cm) flesh-colored cotton fabric for face, head, hands, and upper torso
- 6" × 36" (15.2 × 91.4 cm) tan silk for lower torso and upper arms
- 6" × 18" (15.2 × 45.7 cm) ivory cotton or silk for legs
- 18" × 22" (45.7 × 55.9 cm) Peltex or equivalent
- 18" × 22" (45.7 × 55.9 cm) medium-weight fusible such as HeatnBond
- 18" × 22" (45.7 × 55.9 cm) pastel blue toile or cotton print for skirt
- 9" (22.9 cm) square of tan silk or other fabric for apron
- 2" × 18" (5.1 × 45.7 cm) lace trim for lower skirt edge
- 24" (61 cm) piece of ½" (1.3 cm) -wide trim for the lower skirt (one, two, or more pieces as you desire)
- 24" (61 cm) of trim for sides of the skirt— you can use double fold bias tape or any ½" (1.3 cm) -wide trim
- 6" (15.2 cm) of trim or ribbon for around waist
- 12" (30.5 cm) of narrow ribbon to tie above the lace cuff

*My Marie's colorboard.*    *Hand/Arm variations: top, option 1; bottom, option 2.*

- 8" (20.3 cm) of trim for torso
- ½ yard (45.7 cm) of 1" (2.5 cm) -wide lace for sleeves/cuffs
- 3 yards (2.7 m) of ¼" (6 mm) -wide beige or off-white ribbon for skirt front
- 21 to 24 small buttons, ribbon flowers, or beads to trim skirt front
- optional: 20" (50.8 cm) of ½" (1.3 cm) -wide trim for apron and center chest
- Hair fibers (see page 81 for suggestions)
- fabric inkjet transfer sheet for transferred face
- tacky glue

## PREPARE THE TEMPLATES

Copy the Torso, Head pattern, Head guide, Arm (choose one of the two options), Leg, and Skirt onto card stock, and then carefully cut them out on the line. Remember, Barbara's patterns do not include seam allowances, so trace around the templates on the fabric, and rough-cut the patterns leaving at least 2" (5.1 cm) all around the tracings. You will stitch directly on the traced lines. Another option is to not cut around the tracings until after you have stitched the pieces.

## MAKE THE TORSO AND ARMS

**1.** Pin the tan silk (lower torso) and flesh fabric with right sides together along one longer edge; stitch with a generous ¼" (6 mm) seam allowance. Press the seam allowance toward the darker fabric. Fold the fabric perpendicular to the seam, with right sides facing and the short edges aligned.

**2.** Position the Torso template so the marking on the template aligns with the seam as shown. Trace the template with the purple fade-away marker. **(A)**

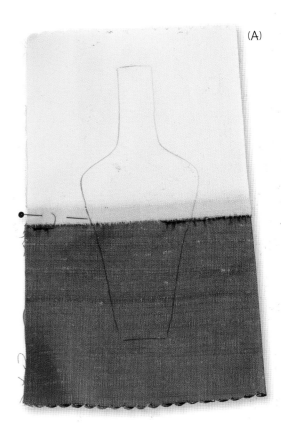

(A)

**3.** Stitch the torso directly on the marked line, leaving the bottom edge unstitched. Cut around the stitching leaving a very generous ¼" (6 mm) seam allowance. Turn the torso right-side out using the hemostats.

## MAKE THE TORSO
## AND ARMS (continued)

**4.** Stuff the torso firmly, particularly the neck (page 19). Whipstitch the bottom edge closed by hand. Glue trim around the chest to cover the seam, overlapping the trim ends at one side (not the center back or center front). You can also glue a trim down the center front of the torso if desired.

**5.** You have two arm options, one with the thumb and one without. Whichever arm you choose, you will want to join two fabrics with a seam above the wrist as instructed for the torso. Position the Arm template so the marking on the template aligns with the seam and the hand is on the flesh-colored fabric. **(B)**

**6.** Trace the template with a mechanical pencil. Note the opening in the back of the arm, and mark the opening lightly on the fabric. Move the template down 2" (5.1 cm) and repeat to trace a second arm.

**7.** Stitch both arms and hands directly on the traced line. For the hand with a thumb, take two stitches across the "V" between the thumb and the mitt as shown. **(C)**

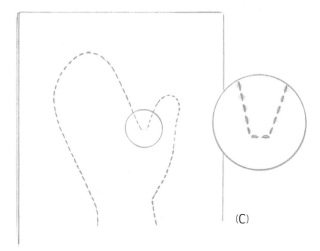

(C)

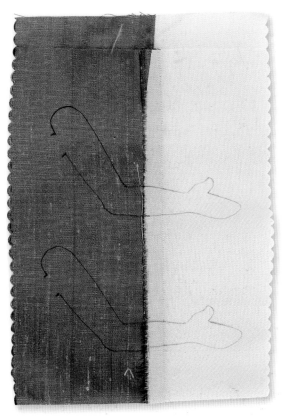

(B)

**8.** Cut around both arms leaving a generous ¼" (6 mm) seam allowance around the arm and a smaller seam allowance around the hand. Carefully clip into the seam allowance at the elbow bend. For the hand with the thumb, clip straight between the thumb and the palm right up to the stitching.

**9.** Turn the hands right-side out using the hemostats. For the hand with the thumb, slip the turning tube inside the arm and into the thumb. Use the rod to press the tip of the thumb firmly against the tube opening. Roll the thumb fabric up onto the rod to turn the thumb. Reach inside the mitt with the hemostats to turn the hand/arm right-side out. (D)

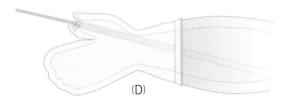

(D)

**10.** Stuff the hands and arms firmly, using the stuffing fork (page 19). Whipstitch the back of the arms closed with matching thread. With nylon thread, slipstitch the arms to the torso, as shown, with several small stitches.

**11.** Cut two 9" (22.9 cm) lengths of lace to make the sleeve cuffs. Hand sew a running stitch along the top edge of the lace with heavy nylon thread to gather the lace. (E)

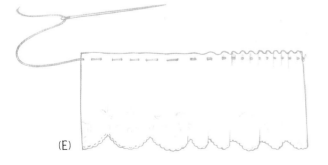

(E)

(F)

**12.** Position a lace cuff around each arm to cover the seam; pull the threads to gather the cuff tight to the arm. Knot the threads securely and bury the tails into the back of the arm. Tie a ribbon just above each lace cuff. Add additional embellishments as desired. (F)

## MAKE THE LEGS AND SKIRT

**1.** Fold the leg fabric in half with the right sides together and trace the Leg template two times with the purple fade-away marker or mechanical pencil. Make sure to leave a generous distance between the tracings.

**2.** Stitch directly on the traced lines, leaving the top edge open on both legs. Cut around the stitching leaving a very generous 1/4" (6 mm) seam allowance.

## MAKE THE LEGS AND SKIRT
### (continued)

**3.** Turn the legs right-side out and stuff firmly to within ½" (1.3 cm) of the top. Whipstitch the top leg openings closed and set them aside. **(G)**

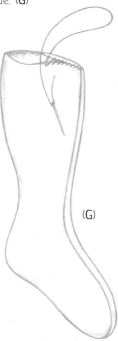

(G)

(H)

**4.** Fuse the HeatnBond to the back of the skirt fabric. Remove the paper backing, and place the adhesive side onto the Peltex; fuse the two layers together.

**5.** Trace the Skirt template twice on the right side of the fabric with the fade-away marker. Cut out the skirts directly on the traced lines. Draw lines on one of the skirt panels to form diamond shapes, as shown on the pattern, with a ruler and the fade-away maker.

**6.** Lay narrow lengths of ribbon over the markings and tack them to the skirt at the points where the ribbons intersect. Sew or glue buttons, flowers, or beads at each of the ribbon intersections, except those on the outer edge of the skirt (those will be attached later).

**7.** Set your sewing machine for a zigzag stitch. Pin the two skirt panels with the wrong sides together, and stitch along the sides over the raw edges, leaving the top and bottom edges open.

**8.** Glue trim on double-fold bias along the front and back sides of the skirt to cover the raw edges. Insert soft layers of fiberfill into the skirt cavity to give the skirt some dimension, but don't overfill or stuff it.

**9.** Pin the legs to the center of the lower skirt edge with the toes pointing outward and heels just barely touching. Machine stitch across the lower edge of the skirt panels catching the legs in the stitching.

**10.** Create a mock shoe by gluing a triangle of lace to the top of each foot and wrapping a ribbon around the ankles. There is no need to cover the bottom of the foot since the lace creates the illusion of a shoe. (H)

**11.** Glue lace trim around the bottom edge of the skirt and then one, two, or more ½" (1.3 cm) -wide trims on top of the lace. Embellish as desired.

**12.** Assemble the doll body by poking the torso down into the upper skirt opening to the waist. Stitch through the waist edge of the skirt and torso from front to back several times.

## MAKE AND ATTACH THE HEAD

**1.** Retrieve the face that you drew or created with the transfer (page 70–73). Make sure you can still see the outline of the face, if necessary retrace the outline using the Feature Placement guide. Copy the slash marking onto the fabric.

**2.** Fold the flesh colored fabric with the right sides together and trace around the head pattern. Place the face with the colored side down onto the doubled head fabric. You will have three layers, one face and two heads. Sew around the head shape on the purple fade-away line. Cut around these pieces leaving a scant ⅛" (3 mm) seam allowance.

(I)

**3.** Slash through only one layer along the marking to create an opening; use a seam ripper or embroidery scissors. (I)

**4.** Turn the head right-side out through the slash. Insert the blunt end of the hemostats into the head and run it along the inside stitched line to smooth the chin curve. Apply a bit of pressure on the seam to help ease and smooth the curve.

**5.** Cut two 2" (5.1 cm) squares of Peltex and glue them together. Lay the head guide template on the Peltex and trace around it with purple fade-away marker. Cut out the Peltex just inside the traced line.

**6.** Put a small amount of glue on one side of the Peltex and slide it inside the slashed opening with the hemostats. Maneuver it all the way down to the chin as far as it will go. This will be the backside of the head and it helps give the face a defined shape.

**7.** With the seam ripper or embroidery scissors, reach inside the slash and cut a smaller opening (half the size of the original slash) through the remaining layer of the head.

## MAKE AND ATTACH THE HEAD
(continued)

**8.** Use the hemostats or stuffing fork to insert small amounts of stuffing through the new opening to fill in the face and give it dimension—keep the texture smooth and don't overfill. Whipstitch the slash openings closed.

**9.** Hand stitch across the foldline indicated on the pattern This creates the back-head flap and holds the face form and fiberfill in place. Fold the top of the head to the back along the foldline, and tack the edges securely. This creates the pocket for the neck stem. (J)

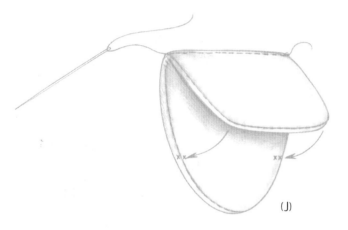

(J)

**10.** Guide a piece of heavy nylon upholstery thread through the fold between the front and back of the head leaving long tails at each end. (K)

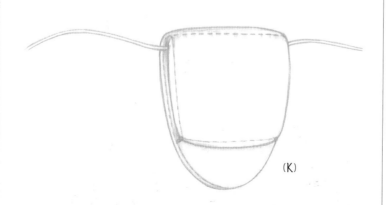

(K)

**11.** Pull the thread tails up and tie them in a tight double knot. Dab a bit of glue over the knot and trim the tails to 2" (5.1 cm) long. This will narrow the top of the head and curve it to make the face/head more dimensional.

**12.** To attach My Marie's head to her body, slide the head onto the neck stem for fit. Find the tilt you like (Barbara usually tilts the head to not look straight on). Remove the head and apply glue to the front and back of the neck stem.

**13.** Slide the head back onto the neck stem, tilt to the desired angle and let the glue dry.

**14.** Choose hair fibers; Tibetan fur that comes on the skin is used for My Marie. (You can also use yarn, mohair or just make a simple hat or head wrap) Cut a strip of fur just big enough to go around her head and about ½" (1.3 cm) wide. Apply glue to the skin side and fold it in half lengthwise. Glue the fur into a circle like a halo, and then glue it in place around her head. Pull the hair up into a ponytail on top of her head and glue small tendrils on each side. **(L)**

(L)

## MAKE THE APRON AND ADD EMBELLISHMENTS

**1.** Cut a 9" (22.9 cm) square of silk or other fabric and fold it into a triangle with the right sides together. Sew the open sides with ¼" (6 mm) seam allowance and leave a 2" (5.1 cm) opening on one side.

**2.** Turn the apron right-side out. Sew a running stitch of heavy nylon thread along the folded edge of the triangle leaving long thread tails at each end.

**3.** Sew or lightly glue the opening closed. Glue optional trim to the apron front along the sides of the triangle, leaving the top untrimmed. Stitch a small tassel to the triangle lower point to finish the apron in true My-Marie fashion. **(M)**

**4.** Place the apron around My Marie's waist, and pull the threads tight so the fullness is in the front, hip to hip. Knot the threads securely in the back and bury the tails. Glue narrow trim around the waist to create a waistband.

**5.** Add beads, buttons and charms as desired to finish your doll.

(M)

# Make Holly

Holly is very similar to My Marie. The simple change to the lower half of the body gives Holly a completely different look. By eliminating the exaggerated hips and adding a center seam, Holly has a more casual look in her comfy lounge pants. Read through the following instructions, as they will often refer back to the instructions for My Marie.

## MATERIALS LIST

- basic doll-making supply kit (page 14)
- specific doll-making and face-painting supplies list (page 15)
- fabric inkjet transfer sheet (for transferred face)
- 1/4 yard (22.9 cm) flesh-colored fabric for face, head, hands, and upper torso
- 1/3 yard (30.5 cm) silk or other rose-colored fabric for upper torso and peplum
- 1/3 yard (30.5 cm) cotton fabric for lounge pants and upper arms
- 6" × 18" (15.2 × 45.7 cm) cotton or silk for legs
- small lace remnants for epaulets
- 12" square (30.5 cm) of Peltex
- 12" square (30.5 cm) of HeatnBond
- 5" × 7" (12.7 × 17.8 cm) Ultrasuede or thin leather for shoes
- variety of ribbons to embellish as desired
- curly mohair yarn for hair
- tacky glue

## PREPARE THE TEMPLATES

Copy the Head pattern, Head guide, Torso, Arm (choose one of two options), Leg, Pants, Peplum and Shoe templates onto card stock and cut them out. Remember Barbara's patterns do not include seam allowances, so trace around the templates on the fabric and rough cut the pieces leaving at least 2" (5.1 cm) all around the tracings. You will stitch directly on the traced lines, unless directed otherwise. Another method is to stitch the pieces on the traced line, and then cut out leaving a 1/4" (6 mm) seam allowance.

## MAKE THE TORSO, ARMS, AND LOWER LEGS

The lounge pants and arms are made from the same cotton print fabric, and the upper torso and peplum are made from the same pink silk.

1. Sew the upper torso, arms, and lower legs just as you did for My Marie (steps 1–10, pages 75–77). This will require sewing the flesh colored fabric to the cotton print for the arms/hands and to the rose fabric for the torso. Glue trim around the arm seams, and add ribbon bows to cover the trim ends.

## MAKE THE PANTS

1. Fuse the HeatnBond onto the back of the lounge pants fabric. Remove the paper backing and fuse it to the Peltex. Trace the Pants template twice on the right side of the fabric with a purple fade-away marker. Cut out the lounge pants on the line.

2. Pin the lounge pants together with wrong sides facing. With matching thread, zigzag the outer edges of the pants from the waist to the lower pant leg edge.

3. Sew a straight-stitch seam on the center marking (refer to template) to create the legs. Darken the stitching line between the legs on the front and back with a colored pencil.

4. Tuck the stuffed lower legs up into the lower pant openings and hand or machine stitch them in place with the toes turned outward.

5. Glue trim along the bottom edge of the pants. Tie two small ribbon bows, and then glue or stitch a bow to the outside of each lower pant leg.

6. Insert lofty pieces of fiberfill into each pant leg and hips from the waist opening to create depth and dimension, but not to fill or wrinkle the shape.

*Holly's colorboard.*

## ASSEMBLE AND
## FINISH HOLLY

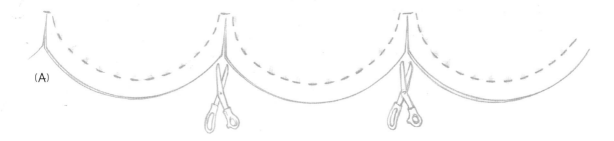

(A)

**1.** Attach the arms to the torso as you did for My Marie (page 77). Gather the top edge of two small pieces of lace edging and stitch them to the shoulders to create epaulets (see Shy, steps 1–2, page 88). Tuck the torso into the waist of the lounge pants and whipstitch them together.

**2.** Fold the peplum fabric with right sides together and position the Peplum template so the foldline on the template is on the fabric fold. Trace the Peplum.

**3.** Stitch carefully along the lines of the marked peplum. Cut the peplum leaving a ½" (1.3 cm) seam allowance. Clip up to the stitching in each scallop point as shown above. (A)

**4.** Make a small slash through one side of the peplum just below the waist edge. Turn the peplum right-side out through the opening. Whipstitch the slash closed, and finger-press the scallops smooth.

**5.** Sew a running stitch (page 18) along the top edge of the peplum with heavy nylon thread. Position the peplum on Holly's waist and pull the threads to gather the peplum to fit around the waist. Knot the threads securely at the center front. Dab tacky glue on the knot and then bury the tails back into the doll. The peplum will not cover her tummy, but will cover her hips and back nicely.

**6.** Glue trim around the waist to cover the top edge of the peplum. Tie bows of decorative ribbon and glue them to the center front. Glue beads down the center front of the torso, and add any other decorative embellishments as desired.

**7.** Fold the shoe leather with right sides together. Place the Shoe pattern on the fold of the leather, and trace around the Shoe template two times. Sew directly on the lines for the heel and top of the shoes (noted by dashed lines below). (B)

(B)

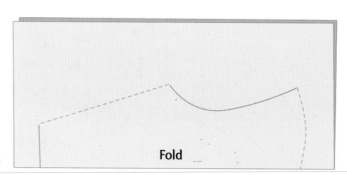

**Fold**

**8.** Cut out the shoes leaving a ⅛" (3 mm) seam allowance from the stitching and directly on the lines that aren't stitched. Glue the seams open along the heel and top of the shoes so they lay flat. Stitch across the heel and toe as shown. **(C)**

(C)

**9.** Trim the corners off the shoes and turn them right-side out. Glue the shoes to the doll's feet and embellish the tops as desired. **(D)**

(D)

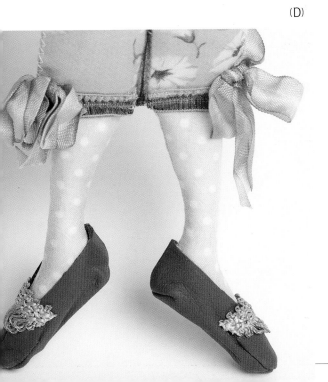

**10.** Make the face (pages 70–73) and make and attach the head to the torso as for My Marie (pages 79–81).

**11.** Wrap small loops of yarn around your hand several times. Thread another piece of yarn through the loops and tie the loops together. Make several yarn bundles. Trim the loops from the untied ends. Glue the tied end of the bundles to Holly's head to cover it completely. Trim the yarn the desired length. **(E)**

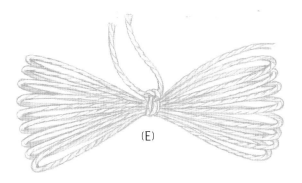

(E)

# Make Shy

A few small changes to the basic doll pattern will turn this fun little design into yet one more doll to complete the trio. This time the torso is lengthened and slightly flared, while the bottom of the doll is tapered and attached to a tail fin.

Shy's lace adornment is from a vintage collar, which was randomly cut up and glued to fabric to create her clothing and tail decoration. Be creative by mixing and matching bits of the lace and trim to cover her upper chest and parts of her tail and fin. The chic trim on her chest is from an old lampshade and the tassel is a piece of upholstery trim (which are the perfect size for doll décor).

## MATERIALS LIST

- basic doll-making supply kit (page 14)
- specific doll-making and face-painting supplies (page 15)
- ¼ yard (22.9 cm) flesh-colored fabric for face, head, arms/hands, and torso
- 10" (25.4 cm) square of printed green cotton fabric for tail
- 16" × 5" (40.6 × 12.7 cm) green velvet or other fabric for fin (save the scraps)
- 12" (30.5 cm) square of Peltex or equivalent
- 12" (30.5 cm) square of HeatnBond or equivalent
- embellishment trims, tassels, glitter, beads, ribbons, and lace
- remnant green tulle
- any fiber hair
- fabric inkjet transfer sheet (for transferred face)
- tacky glue

## PREPARE THE TEMPLATES

Copy the Head pattern, Head guide, Torso, Arm (choose one of the two options), Tail, Fin, and Sleeve Cap templates onto card stock and cut them out. Remember Barbara's patterns do not include seam allowances, so trace around the templates on the fabric and rough cut the pieces leaving at least 2" (5.1 cm) all around the tracings. You will stitch directly on the traced lines, unless directed otherwise. Another method is to stitch the pieces on the traced line, and then cut out leaving a ¼" (6 mm) seam allowance.

## MAKE THE TORSO AND ARMS

1. Fold the flesh-colored fabric with right sides together and trace the torso once and the arms two times onto the fabric. Refer to sewing the torso and arms for My Marie (steps 3–4, pages 75–76; steps 7–10, page 76).

## •••• TIP

If you want, bend one arm slightly at the elbow, and tack it in place on the inner elbow with a needle and thread to keep the arm bent.

## MAKE THE TAIL AND FIN

1. Fold the tail fabric with right sides together and trace around the Tail template. Stitch on the traced line leaving the top edge unstitched. Cut out the tail, leaving a ½" (1.3 cm) seam allowance. Turn the tail right-side out.

2. Finger-press the top raw edges ½" (1.3 cm) to the inside. Fold a small horizontal pleat close to the top edge in the center front; hand stitch the pleat closed. (A)

(A)

*Shy's colorboard.*

## MAKE THE TAIL AND FIN
**(continued)**

**3.** Fold the fin fabric with right sides together, and trace around the Fin template. Stitch on the traced lines around the curved edges, leaving the straight top edge unstitched. Cut out the fin, around the stitching with a ½" (1.3 cm) seam allowance. Clip into each scallop up to the stitching, and then turn the fin right-side out. Lightly stuff the fin and set it aside.

**4.** Insert fiberfill into the tail from the top opening to fill the lower part of the tail up to the dotted line (see template). Machine or hand stitch across the dotted line to keep the stuffing in place.

**5.** Softly stuff the rest of the tail. Slide the tail onto the torso and pinch pleat the back opening so it fits the back torso. Whipstitch the torso to the tail.

**6.** Slide the fin onto the bottom of the tail and pin it in place. Tuck the top raw edges of the fin to the inside and whipstitch the fin securely onto the bottom of the tail.

**7.** Hand sew vertical stitching lines on the fin as indicated on the template.

## ASSEMBLE AND FINISH SHY

**1.** Attach the arms to the torso as you did for My Marie (step 10, page 77). Trace the sleeve cap template two times on the wrong side of the velvet. Cut the sleeve caps on the marked lines. Sew a running stitch across the top edge of each, leaving long thread tails.

**2.** Wrap the sleeve caps over each shoulder and pull the threads to gather the shoulder edges. Knot the threads under the arms and bury the thread tails. Wrap a small strip of green tulle around each arm just below the sleeve caps. (B)

(B)

(C)

**6.** Glue hair fibers to cover the head. Any type of hair fiber will be lovely. (Barbara used her favorite shade of Tibetan skin for the hair and glued small strips to cover the head.)

**7.** Make the seaweed cap by cutting a strip of leftover velvet approximately 2" × 5" (5.1 × 12.7 cm). Sew a running stitch along one long edge and pull the threads to gather it tight. Knot the threads securely. Cut deep notches into the lower edge of the velvet, and glue or pin the cap to Shy's head. (D)

(D)

**3.** Make the face (pages 72–73) with a slight variation for Shy's downcast eyes. Notice that only the lower half of the football shape was drawn in with black Pigma pen. With the mechanical pencil, draw a football shape around the eye dot to create the outer line. Directly over the inked line draw another half football shape, leaving a ¹⁄₁₆" (1.6 mm) slit between the two lines. Go over the pencil lines with a black Pigma pen. Draw a very small iris with blue or green gel pen off to one side in each eye as shown. (C)

**4.** Shade and highlight the upper eyelids with colored pencils. Shade each side of the upper eyelid, leaving the center white to create the effect of the rounded eyeball beneath the eyelid. Add more shading with colored pencils or powdered eye shadows.

**5.** Make and attach the head (pages 79–80) to the torso as you did for My Marie.

**8.** Lots of trim and lace are used to add fun to the costume, and all are glued securely to her with the exception of the tassel at the bottom of her fin, which is tacked sercurely in place. Add some glitter glue to her cheeks and body to give her a just-out-of-the-ocean look.

# GALLERY
## elinor peace bailey

## ALL OF ME

(above)  This is a painting I did when I was a student.
My mother had claimed it, but when my sister,
Marie Fay, moved in with me, she brought it with
her. The painting reminds me of how little I have
really changed. I still love the variety of children
that play upon its surface; I am still there.

# A FAIRY CASTLE—
# A TRIBUTE TO THE
# MEN IN MY LIFE

(right) When out walking the property of a retreat house in Minnesota, I spotted a charming castle of found wooden objects that captured my imagination. The hunt began to create my own—only larger. The castle began to take shape when Gary and I found a sturdy box at a high desert antique shop in California while on our way to Arizona to visit our son Isaac and his family. Isaac, who also photographs my world, built the base and crown of the box. Frank Kiraly, a friend and contractor, donated his thirty-year-old nail box. Rich Ohare of Lincoln, Nebraska, who also built our new bathroom, sent me the newel post, which he had freshly varnished. Christian Fox, my dear son-in-law, provided the tower to top the construction. An old hinge and a fence top came from The Little House in Three Rivers, Michigan, where I spent many summers as a child. I added two type drawers and hundreds of miniatures I had gathered over the years. As a final touch, my own true love marched into the woods and collected two Man- zanita branches (his favorite evergreen tree) for the top of the castle. This piece resides in my library in Vancouver.

## THE VICTORIAN DOLL—AGAIN AND AGAIN AND AGAIN

(opposite)  The very first doll that I created a pattern for was The Victorian Doll, shown here in three of countless variations. I have sold nearly 20,000 copies of this pattern through the years and many of my students still show up to class prepared to make their first doll in Victorian style. This doll is not complicated and is primitive in style, but I could not design her today, as I know too much to be satisfied with the simple techniques she was born from. In the three hundred, or so, times that I have reproduced her, she still continues to give me pleasure.

## GOOD OLD BOY—TIMES TWO

(above)  This doll is a tribute to Gary, the man who shaped so much of my life by providing me the freedom to find my own way. The Good Old Boy not only has a western reference, but is also a treasured family name. And because Gary played the saxophone, the Good Old Boy does, too. Today, the Good Old Boy doll is available as a pattern, which can be translated into many different characters. To me, the Good Old Boy is just Gary being himself.

## JOURNALS

**(above)** For about ten years, I have kept art journals. As I tell my students, "I lead a personal, but not a private life." My focus point is the figure, old postcards, and other paper treasures. I alter an old book with gesso painted onto the pages. I add various items from my paper collection and then enter words and embellish with figures. I use a variety of graphic supplies, which I collect. These books are filled with the ideas that I am developing.

## DRAWING OUT OF THE BOX

**(opposite)** This complex piece is a treasure trove of my thoughts and aspirations. My personal myth is written on the inside, and my journey to doll making is stitched on the outside. The bottom features a giant stamped message that reads, "I am me for that I came." All of these words and fabric art ride on the back of a crawling figure, symbolic of the tortoise on whose back sits the world. It must be apparent by now that I am a self-proclaimed navel gazer and consider my art very self-centered.

# GALLERY
## Patti Medaris Culea

### PATTI WITH SUSAN DRAWING A DOLL'S FACE

**(top)** Most of my teaching is done in a workshop setting when I'm on trips to various shops and guilds. At home, my studio is small but large enough to teach up to three people. When I'm at home, I love teaching because all my "stuff" is close at hand.

### PATTI WITH HER QUILT

**(above)** Curves and sculpting are the predominant features of my art; however, I have also found great enjoyment in creating things that are flat. For more than a year, I've been working on this quilt. I can "flat out" tell you it was a major learning experience. The quilt has been a personal journey as it reflects many of the dolls in my pattern line who also are part of my family.

## FIVE DOLLS CREATED
## BY FIVE STUDENTS

(above) I'm proud to share these dolls that were created by people who attended my workshops or who read my other books. From left to right, they are as follows:

Daisey Mae was made by Ellen Juhl from Boca Raton, Florida. Ellen has taken several of my workshops over the years and is now an accomplished doll maker.

Lydia is a doll made by Marla Tomlinson of Navarre, Florida. Marla used my books to teach herself the basics of doll making. She is a relatively new doll maker, however you can see her strong background in watercolor and mixed media.

Journey is ready to travel around the world. Her creator is Abi Monroe of Tuscola, Texas. Abi was born in England and moved to the United States in 2008. She shows great promise after just one year of making dolls. I am honored that Abi's inspiration came from my first book, *Creative Cloth Doll Making*, and can't wait to see her future work.

Asaylatine is the creation of Candice Ratcliff Sinclair. Candice started making dolls when she was 10 years old and entered 4-H competitions. Candice lives in Rensselaer, Indiana, and as you can see from her doll, she loves fashion. Candice recently received a Bachelor of Science degree in Apparel Design and Fashion Merchandising.

Professional doll maker Susan Barmore, of Frowning Francis Pattern Company created Raven. Susan usually is known for her primitive dolls; however, we are pleased to have her venture into the world of fantasy dolls. Raven's unique techniques can be seen in her clothing. The wings are made from fused grocery bags; her skirt from recycled dryer sheets, and the shoes and halter from unused baby wipes. Talk about going green!

## PATTI'S BEADED DOLL

(left) I have always loved beading, whether it's embellishing a doll or creating a beaded pin; beading is therapeutic for me. This is a beading-sample doll. I applied many beading techniques on her and have used the doll in workshops over the years.

## PATTI'S FANS

**(above)** Paper dolls were an important part of the childhood I never grew out of. When elinor extended a challenge to create something from the theme "Opposites Attract," my idea was to create a fan with a paper doll on each blade. The clothes are removable so the dolls can wear different outfits.

## MIKAELA AND LIZZY

**(right)** Mikaela and Lizzy are samples from one of my patterns, and Mikaela is my answer to the popular ball-jointed dolls. The ball joints enables the doll to sit and make a variety of poses.

## MARLY

(right) An idea I had when writing
doll-making books for Quarry Books
was to use the same-size doll in each
book so people could mix and match
body parts and create their own doll.
Marly is a sample of that technique and
is made from body parts from *Creative
Cloth Doll Making* and *Creative Cloth
Doll Faces*.

# GALLERY
## Barbara Willis

## MEMORY-BOX DOLL

**(above)** I wanted to enjoy some of the little treasures that I have tucked out of sight in drawers and cupboards by incorporating them into a doll. I have many lovely little reminders of life's pleasures, such as family photos, souvenirs from trips abroad, my aunt's rouge pot, and a small sewing box with my grandmother's thimble.

So with inspiration and a goal, I removed the lid from an old cigar box, cut the lid in half and reattached it to create a cupboard with two doors.

I then began constructing the doll; a process that I loved. I had to figure out how to attach her dress around the box as if it really belonged there. A wee bit of fantasy and a lot of fun went into the finished doll. I used rubber stamps to add the design on her silk dress, created shoes with turned-up toes and created a special heart for her to hold close.

The doll now hangs on the wall of my studio, and every time I pass her I'm reminded of lovely times gone by.

## A CHILD IS BORN

(above)  This lovely little announcement was inspired by the birth of my first grandchild. Katrina Hailey came into our lives full of sugar and spice and all things nice. I hope one day to use this doll on the cover of a memory book or journal I plan to create for Katrina. In the meantime it's a lovely way to honor her birth and welcome her into the family.

I love fabric and all things pretty, so this was a perfect way to use some special lace and ribbons I'd been saving. I used a pair of vintage-earring findings as the hanger and connected them together with a small crown charm. I couldn't dream of a better way to use those special buttons I had stashed away!

## FRENCH FASHION DOLL

(above)  I love French fashion images from the 1830s. I have been making a series of these fashion mavens using bits of favorite fabrics, laces and trims. I copied the image onto a fabric sheet using my inkjet printer, but used only the head and feet. I then created an elongated torso and arms out of several layers of fabric, Peltex, and decorative paper. Once I had the parts redesigned, I got busy and played, pulling out silk fabrics, velvet ribbons, vintage flowers, Victorian laces, and some lovely French ribbon.

## DELIGHT

**(left)** Delight is a stump doll, meaning she has
no legs, but is tall enough to look as if she might
have a pair hiding under the long skirt and silk
jacket. If she had legs, I surely would have added
stunning shoes!

I created Delight by first sculpting a face from
polymer clay. Then I created a mold and pressed
in a paper-clay impression. When the impression
was dry, I cleaned the mask and covered it with
a fine gauge knit fabric that matched the woven
fabric I intended to use for the chest and hands.

This is a doll technique I teach in one of my
workshops. I think it's always so fun to watch the
dolls and their makers as they form an unmis-
takable likeness to one another—like mother like
daughter, as they say.

I love that this doll is delicate, feminine, and just
a *Delight*.

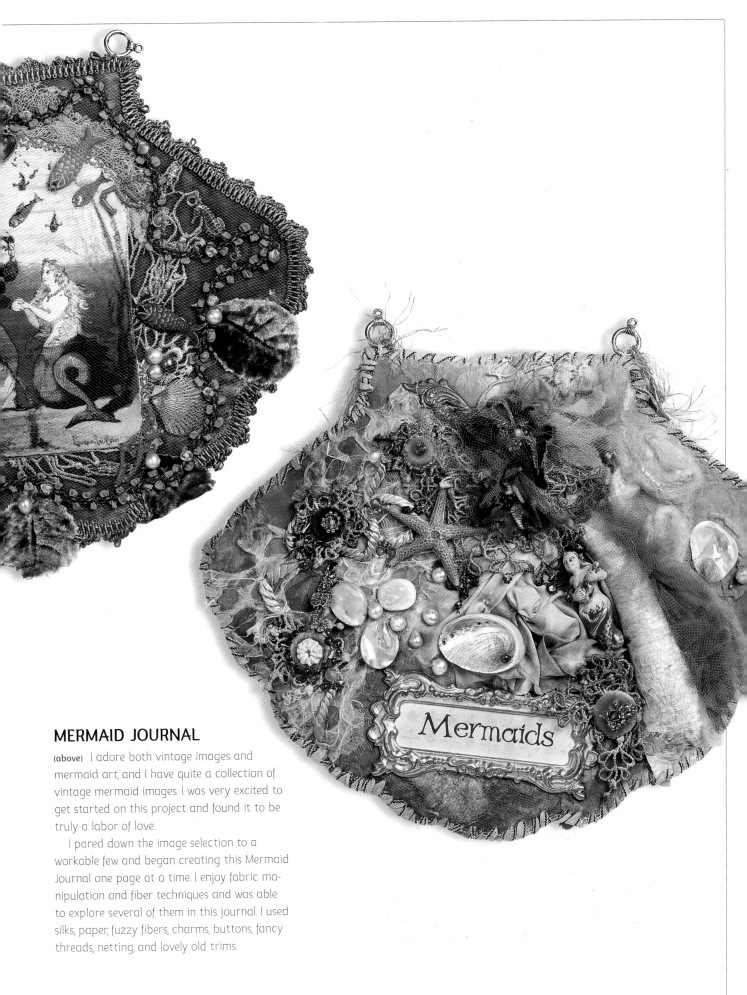

## MERMAID JOURNAL

**(above)** I adore both vintage images and mermaid art, and I have quite a collection of vintage mermaid images. I was very excited to get started on this project and found it to be truly a labor of love.

I pared down the image selection to a workable few and began creating this Mermaid Journal one page at a time. I enjoy fabric manipulation and fiber techniques and was able to explore several of them in this journal. I used silks, paper, fuzzy fibers, charms, buttons, fancy threads, netting, and lovely old trims.

## SHORE MAIDEN

**(above)** The Shore Maiden features a soft sculpted face technique that is my favorite when making my dolls. I enjoy the flexibility of the knit fabric as I move and manipulate it to create depth and expression with each stitch. You can learn about this technique in depth in my earlier publication, *Cloth Doll Artistry*, also published by Quarry Books.

Sculpting the face can be challenging, and it definitely takes a determined doll maker to yield to the learning curve of this technique, but the necessary focus and patience pays off. I enjoy the learning process because it teaches me to never feel as if I have failed. I feel that I gain better knowledge and control of the technique with each stitch.

## CHELSEA

Chelsea is a lovely doll created from a stable woven cotton fabric. Although woven cotton doesn't yield as much to depth and manipulation as does a knit fabric, it can still create doll magic. With a few darts on the chin and forehead to create dimension and by coloring on the face, this doll has the appearance of fully developed features.

My passion for fabrics, trims, and ribbons is lovingly lavished on my doll creations—Chelsea is no exception. I enjoyed creating every inch of her as I went through the process of picking and choosing her final costume fabrics.

## SEW LOVELY

This exquisite wall hanging was inspired by my love of sewing. A bit of fabric, a few old sewing notions, and an old button card were just waiting to become this decorative reminder of things I enjoy.

# Patterns for Ginger

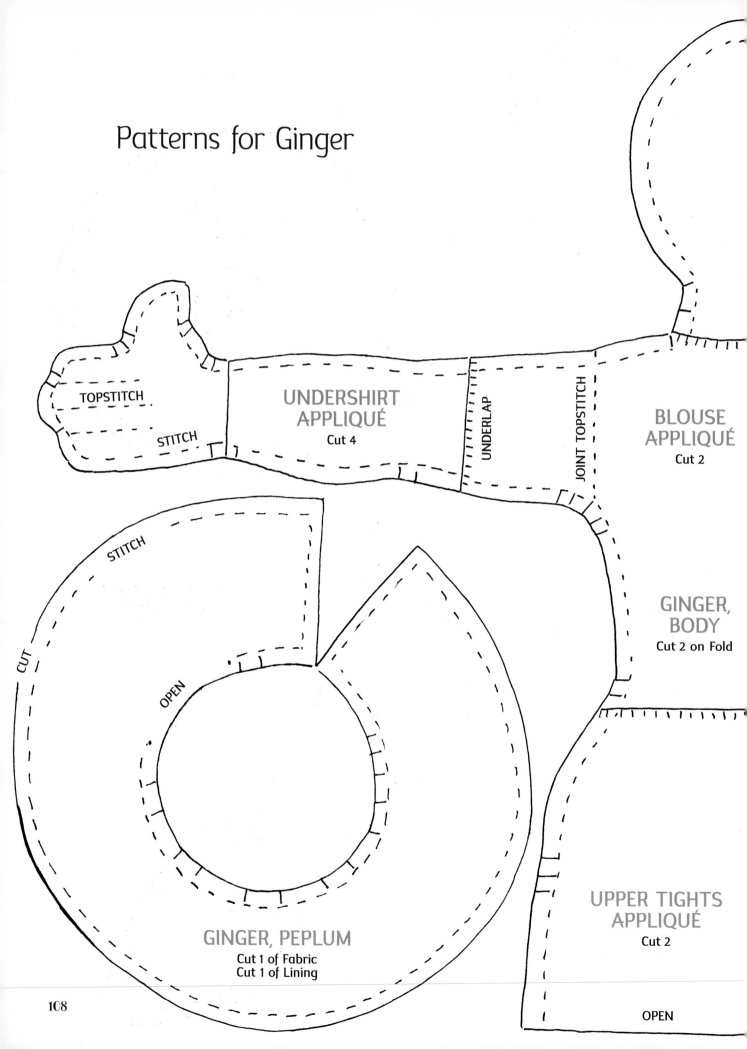

TOPSTITCH

STITCH

UNDERSHIRT
APPLIQUÉ
Cut 4

UNDERLAP

JOINT TOPSTITCH

BLOUSE
APPLIQUÉ
Cut 2

STITCH

CUT

OPEN

GINGER,
BODY
Cut 2 on Fold

GINGER, PEPLUM
Cut 1 of Fabric
Cut 1 of Lining

UPPER TIGHTS
APPLIQUÉ
Cut 2

OPEN

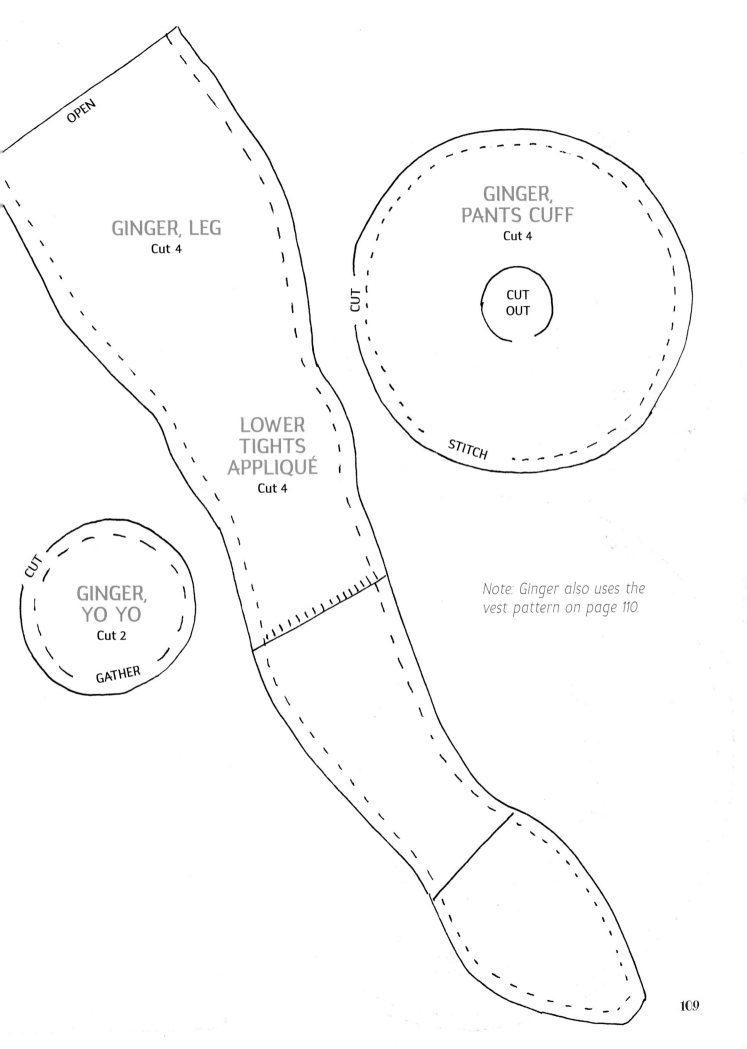

OPEN

**GINGER, LEG**
Cut 4

**GINGER,
PANTS CUFF**
Cut 4

CUT

CUT
OUT

STITCH

**LOWER
TIGHTS
APPLIQUÉ**
Cut 4

CUT

**GINGER,
YO YO**
Cut 2

GATHER

*Note: Ginger also uses the
vest pattern on page 110.*

# Patterns for Gypsy

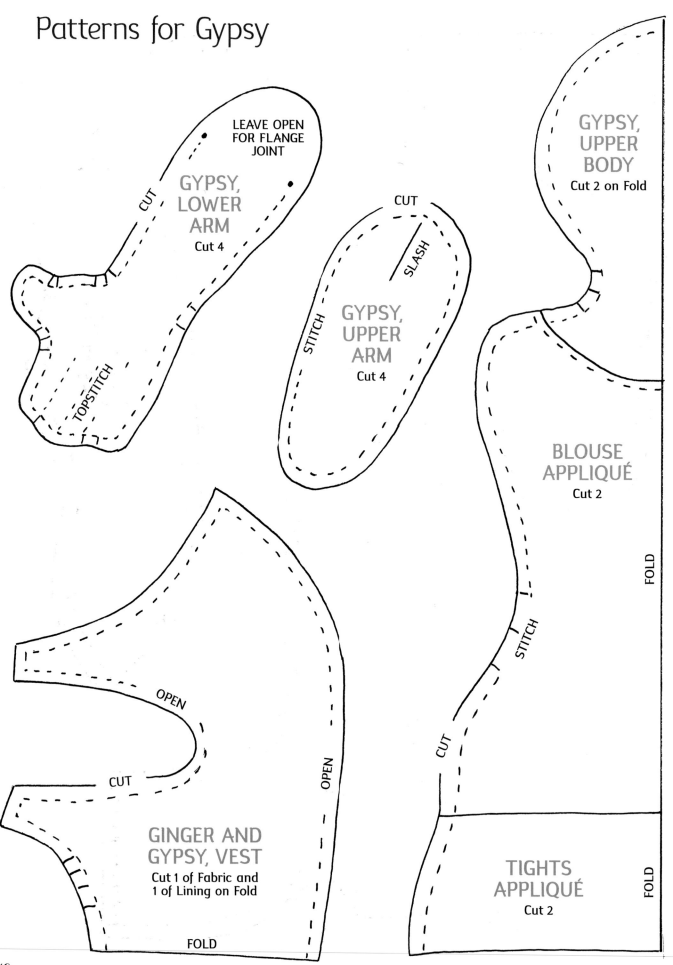

LEAVE OPEN
FOR FLANGE
JOINT

GYPSY,
LOWER
ARM

Cut 4

CUT

TOPSTITCH

CUT

STITCH

SLASH

GYPSY,
UPPER
ARM

Cut 4

GYPSY,
UPPER
BODY

Cut 2 on Fold

BLOUSE
APPLIQUÉ

Cut 2

FOLD

STITCH

CUT

OPEN

CUT

OPEN

GINGER AND
GYPSY, VEST

Cut 1 of Fabric and
1 of Lining on Fold

FOLD

TIGHTS
APPLIQUÉ

Cut 2

FOLD

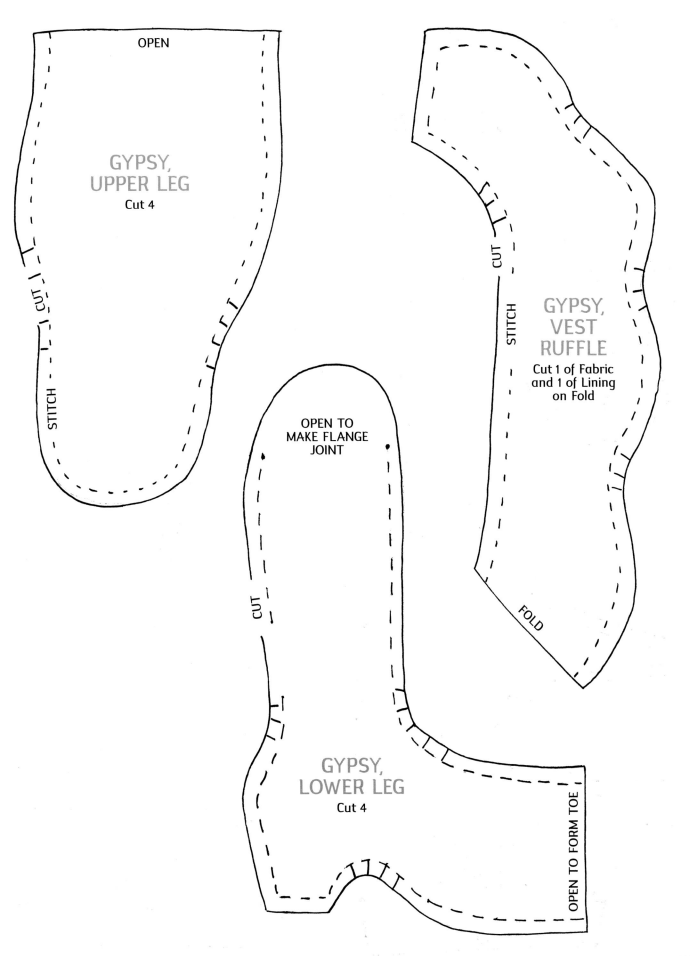

OPEN

GYPSY,
UPPER LEG
Cut 4

STITCH CUT

GYPSY,
VEST
RUFFLE

Cut 1 of Fabric
and 1 of Lining
on Fold

STITCH CUT

FOLD

OPEN TO
MAKE FLANGE
JOINT

CUT

GYPSY,
LOWER LEG
Cut 4

OPEN TO FORM TOE

111

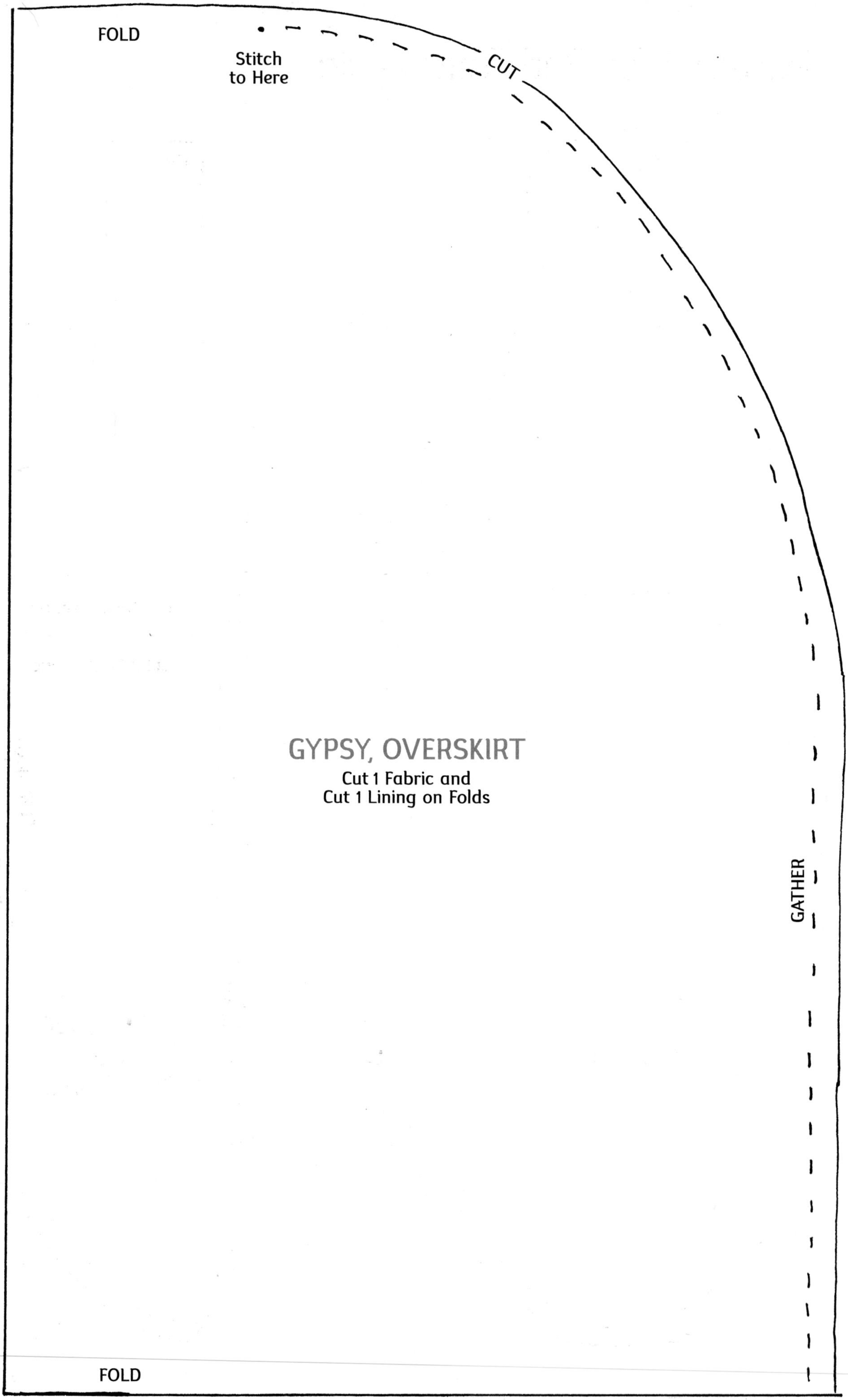

FOLD

Stitch
to Here

CUT

GYPSY, OVERSKIRT

Cut 1 Fabric and
Cut 1 Lining on Folds

GATHER

FOLD

FOLD

# Patterns for Beth and Lydia

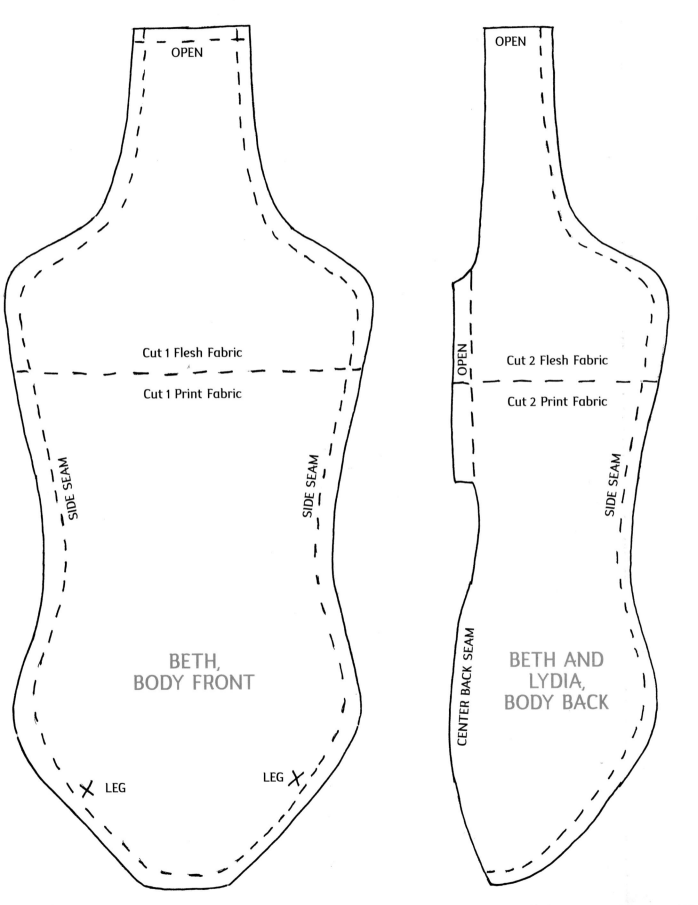

OPEN

Cut 1 Flesh Fabric

Cut 1 Print Fabric

SIDE SEAM

SIDE SEAM

BETH,
BODY FRONT

LEG

LEG

OPEN

OPEN

Cut 2 Flesh Fabric

Cut 2 Print Fabric

SIDE SEAM

CENTER BACK SEAM

BETH AND
LYDIA,
BODY BACK

# Patterns for Beth and Lydia

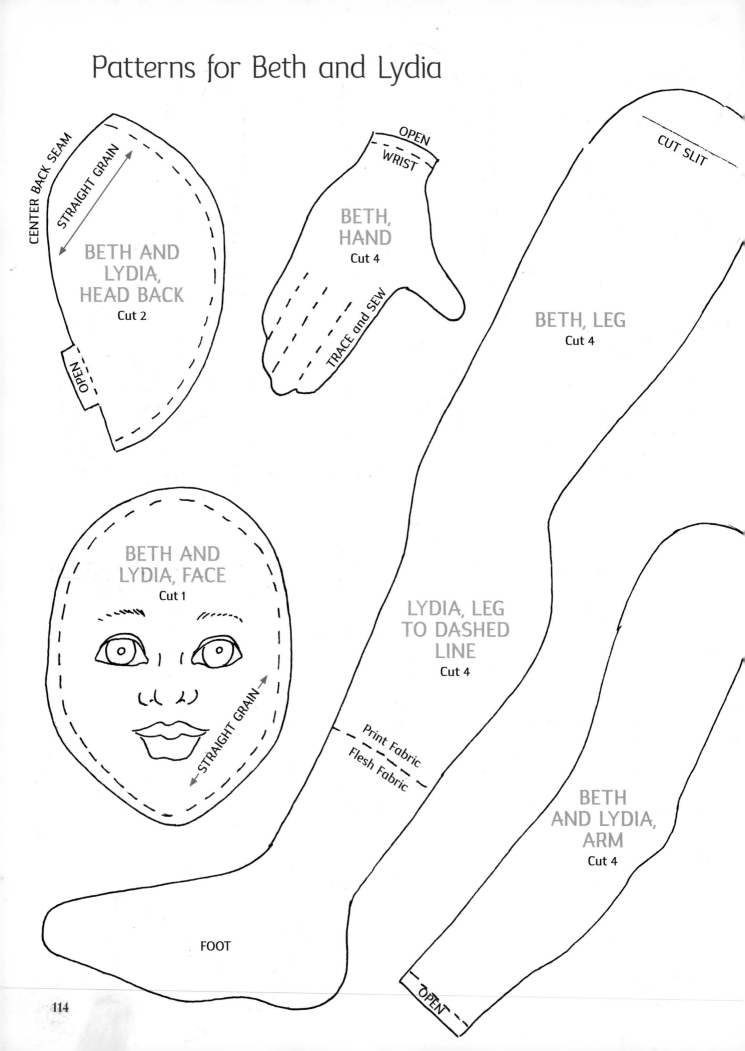

CENTER BACK SEAM

STRAIGHT GRAIN

**BETH AND LYDIA, HEAD BACK**
Cut 2

OPEN

OPEN

WRIST

**BETH, HAND**
Cut 4

TRACE and SEW

CUT SLIT

**BETH, LEG**
Cut 4

**BETH AND LYDIA, FACE**
Cut 1

STRAIGHT GRAIN

**LYDIA, LEG TO DASHED LINE**
Cut 4

Print Fabric

Flesh Fabric

**BETH AND LYDIA, ARM**
Cut 4

FOOT

OPEN

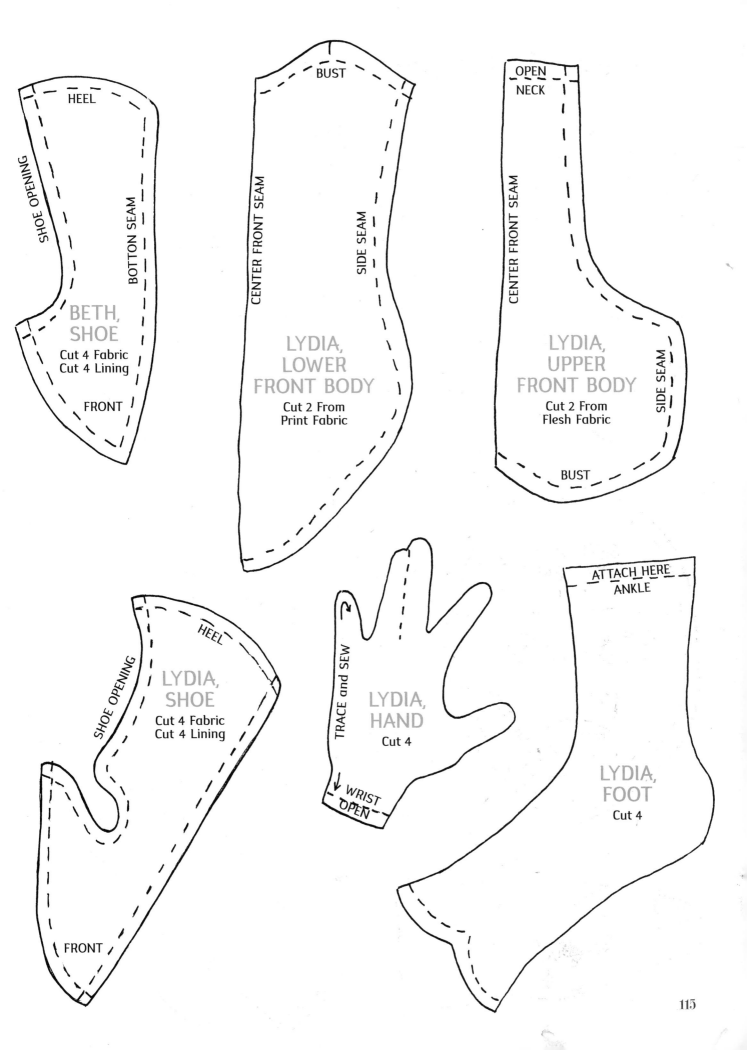

HEEL

SHOE OPENING

BOTTON SEAM

**BETH, SHOE**

Cut 4 Fabric
Cut 4 Lining

FRONT

BUST

CENTER FRONT SEAM

SIDE SEAM

**LYDIA, LOWER FRONT BODY**

Cut 2 From Print Fabric

OPEN

NECK

CENTER FRONT SEAM

SIDE SEAM

**LYDIA, UPPER FRONT BODY**

Cut 2 From Flesh Fabric

BUST

HEEL

SHOE OPENING

**LYDIA, SHOE**

Cut 4 Fabric
Cut 4 Lining

FRONT

TRACE and SEW

**LYDIA, HAND**

Cut 4

WRIST OPEN

ATTACH HERE

ANKLE

**LYDIA, FOOT**

Cut 4

115

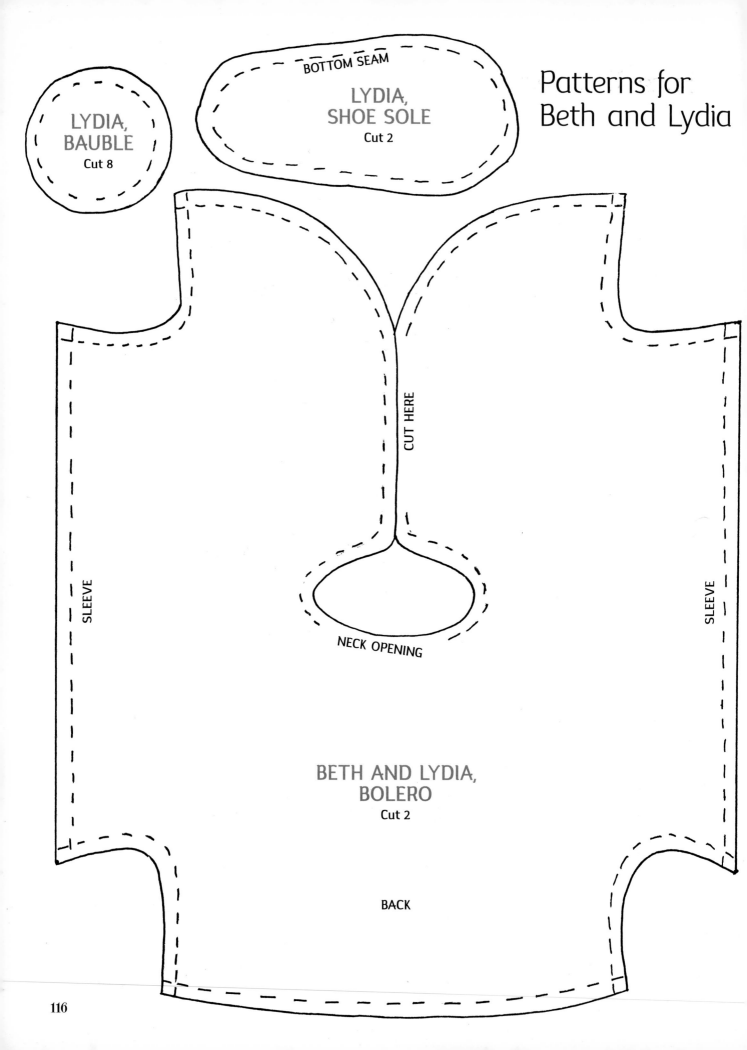

LYDIA,
BAUBLE
Cut 8

BOTTOM SEAM

LYDIA,
SHOE SOLE
Cut 2

Patterns for
Beth and Lydia

CUT HERE

SLEEVE

SLEEVE

NECK OPENING

BETH AND LYDIA,
BOLERO
Cut 2

BACK

# Face Transfers

MY MARIE

HOLLY

SHY

# Patterns for My Marie, Holly, and Shy

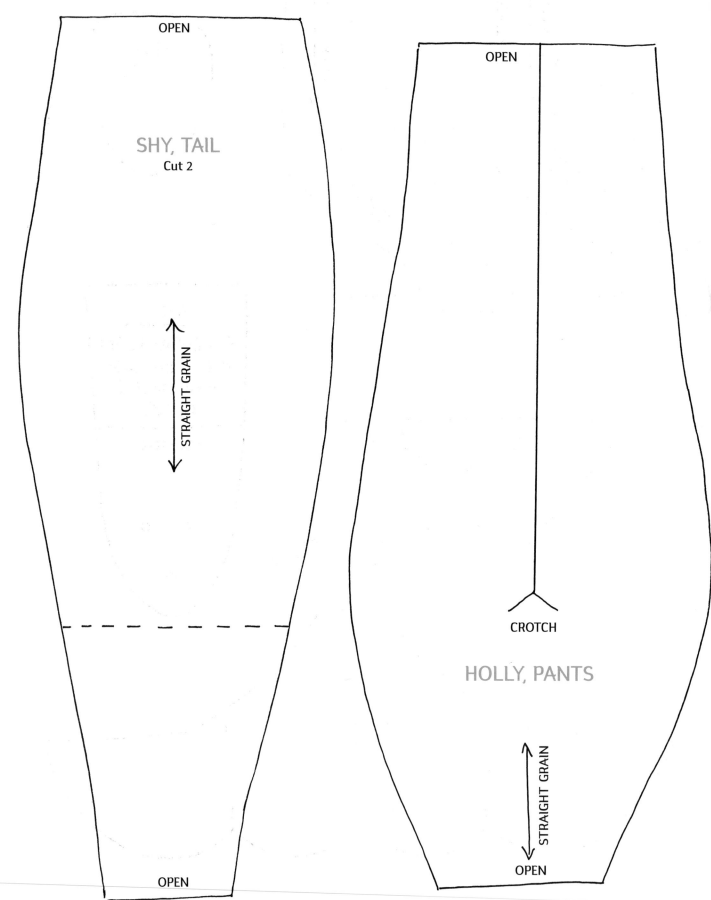

OPEN

SHY, TAIL
Cut 2

STRAIGHT GRAIN

OPEN

OPEN

CROTCH

HOLLY, PANTS

STRAIGHT GRAIN

OPEN

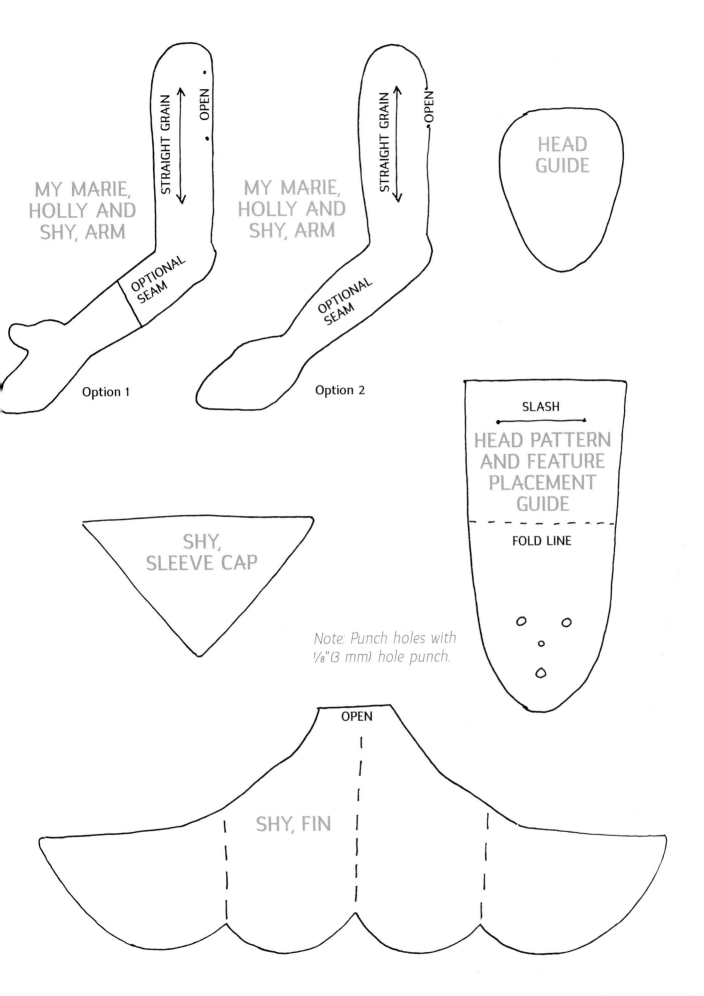

MY MARIE, HOLLY AND SHY, ARM

STRAIGHT GRAIN

OPEN

OPTIONAL SEAM

Option 1

MY MARIE, HOLLY AND SHY, ARM

STRAIGHT GRAIN

OPEN

OPTIONAL SEAM

Option 2

HEAD GUIDE

SHY, SLEEVE CAP

*Note: Punch holes with ⅛"(3 mm) hole punch.*

SLASH

HEAD PATTERN AND FEATURE PLACEMENT GUIDE

FOLD LINE

OPEN

SHY, FIN

# Patterns for My Marie, Holly, and Shy

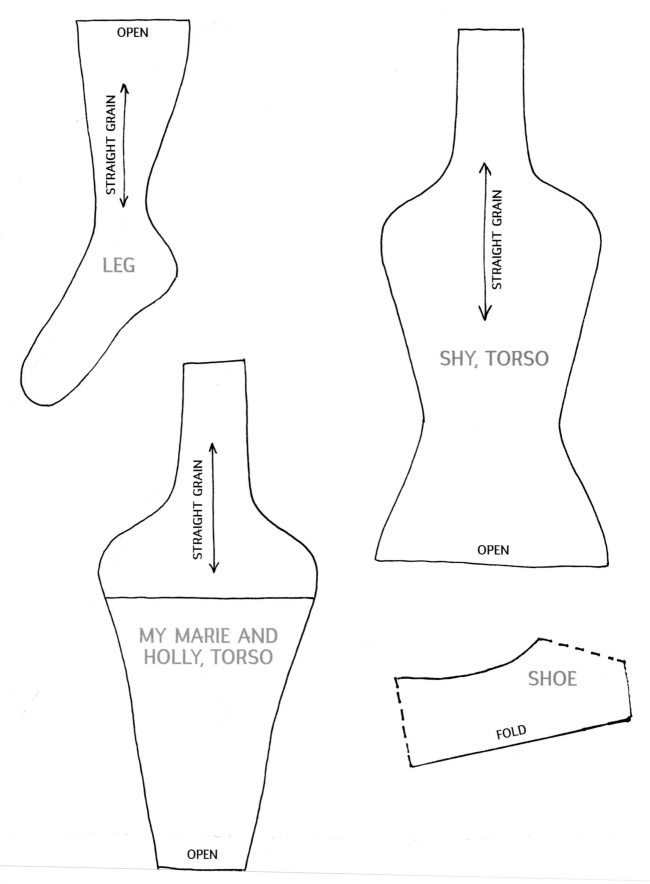

OPEN

STRAIGHT GRAIN

LEG

STRAIGHT GRAIN

SHY, TORSO

OPEN

STRAIGHT GRAIN

MY MARIE AND
HOLLY, TORSO

OPEN

SHOE

FOLD

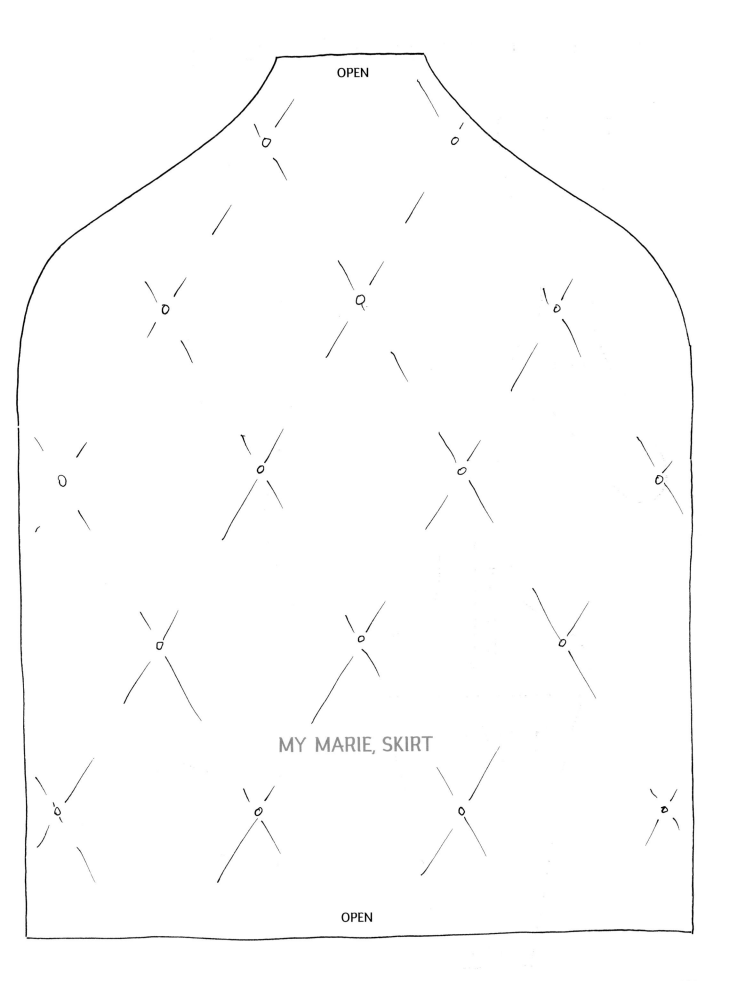

OPEN

MY MARIE, SKIRT

OPEN

# Pattern for Holly

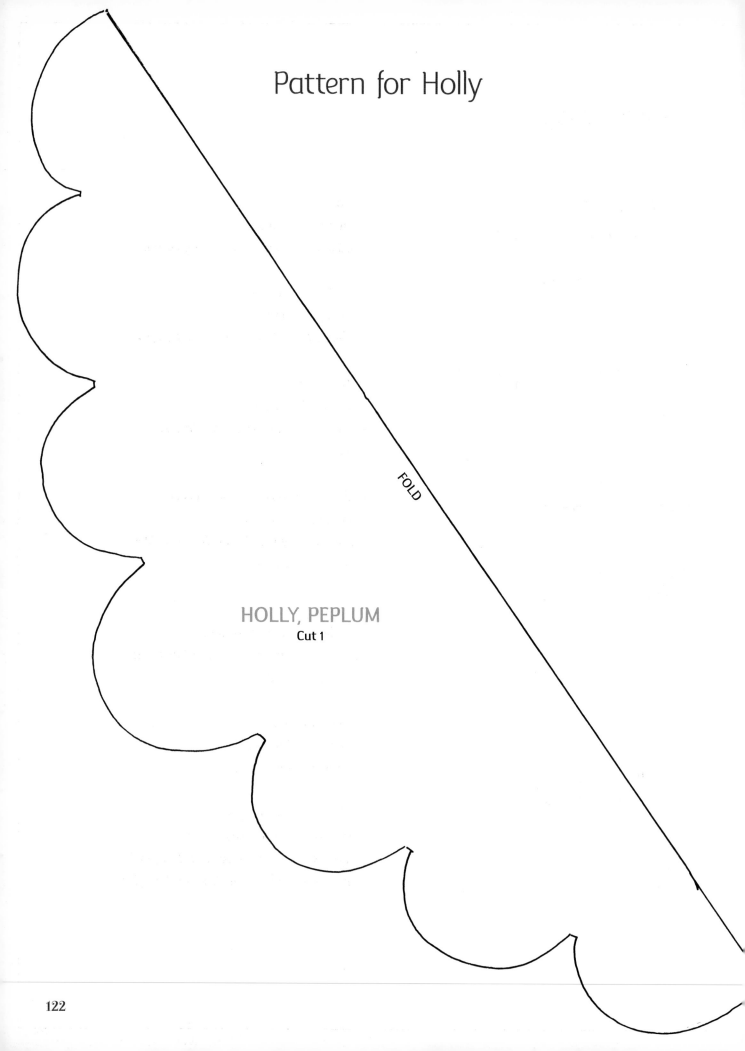

FOLD

HOLLY, PEPLUM
Cut 1

# Resources

## United States

elinor peace bailey
www.epbdolls.com
*Turn-it-all tools, patterns, fabrics, classes*

Cloth Doll Connection
www.clothdollconnection.com
*Online doll-making classes, links, events*

Collett Fenske Fabric
146 Kelsey Lane
Myers Flat, CA 95554
collett@asis.com
*Hand-dyed and over-dyed checks
and ticking*

Craft Warehouse
www.Craftwarehouse.com
*Scrapbooking supplies and notions*

Dharma Trading Company
www.dharmatrading.com
*Supplies for dying fabric*

Dollmaker's Journey
www.dollmakersjourney.com
*Patterns, fabrics, doll hair, tools*

Joggles, Inc.
www.joggles.com
*Patterns, fabrics, beads, books, mohair,
fibers*

Meinke Toy
www.meinketoy.com
*Books, threads, stabilizers, Angelina fibers*

M and J Trimmings
www.mjtrim.com
*Ribbons, trims, beads, crystals, buttons*

PMC Designs
www.pmcdesigns.com
*Patterns, tools, newsletters, classes,
rubber stamps*

Quilting Arts/Cloth Paper Scissors
www.quiltingarts.com
*Jacquard products, books, beads, rubber
stamps, magazines*

Rupert Gibbon & Spider
www.jacquardproducts.com
*Jacquard products: Dye-NA-Flow paints,
Lumiere paints, textile paints*

Tsukineko, Inc.
www.tsukineko.com
*Fantastix, stamp pads*

Barbara Willis Designs
www.barbarawillisdesigns.com
*Original cloth doll designs, stuffing forks,
pima cotton body fabric, Tibetan hair fibers*

## Canada

Opus Framing & Arts
www.opusframing.com
*Jacquard products, books, workshops*

## Australia

Anne's Glory Box
www.annesglorybox.com.au
*Fabrics, dyes, paints, beads, books, stabilizers, mohair*

Fabric Additions
Fabricaddictions.com
*Tools, workshops, books, and stuffing forks*

The Thread Studio
www.thethreadstudio.com
*Threads, stabilizers, paints, books, beads, online classes*

## New Zealand

Zig Zag
www.2dye4.co.nz
*Jacquard products, rubber stamps, Prismacolor pencils*

## United Kingdom

Art Van Go
www.artvango.co.uk
*Jacquard products, Stewart Gill Paints, books*

Crafty Notions
www.craftynotions.com
*Stabilizers, paints, Angelina fibres, beads, bead supplies, books*

Fibrecrafts & George Weil
www.fibrecrafts.com
*Paints, Angelina, books, workshops*

Jan Horrox Cloth Doll Supplies
www.jan-horrox.com
*Full line of patterns, cloth doll supplies, tools*

Rainbow Silks
www.rainbowsilks.co.uk
*Jacquard products, beads, books, classes, rubber stamps, embossing powders, tools*

## Europe

Bernina Creative Center
Bubenecska 43
Prague 6, Czech Republic
www.bernina-dani.cz
*Jacquard products, beads, books, patterns, threads, machines, classes*

# Acknowledgments

### elinor peace bailey

I give thanks to the friends and family who sustain me as an artist. The two doll makers that worked on this book with me have been wonderful companions for several years. We've plotted and planned dozens of projects together, but with as much imagination as we have as a collective group we don't have much organization. Thank goodness for the small army at Quarry Books who gave our ideas order. I also give my personal thanks to my son, Isaac Bailey, who is such a gifted photographer and generous enough to work with his mother.

## PATTI MEDARIS CULEA

Without Mary Ann Hall's dream, this book would not be possible. After she approached me with the idea of a basic book on doll making and collaborating with friends, elinor peace bailey and Barbara Willis, I caught her vision.

As often happens, travel schedules and family demands get in the way of a project. Such was the case with this book; yet Mary Ann kept us focused and on target. Juggling three authors with entirely different personalities was mission almost impossible, but she gently brought everything together.

My husband, John provided the encouragement and "barking" to keep me on track for each deadline. I'm especially thankful to Bob and Susan Hirsch whose expertise made our photo sessions a visual triumph. Bob has been my photographer for about twenty years. He knows my style and Susan has a special knack for display.

And finally, my deepest gratitude goes to you for holding this book in your hands and hopefully adding it to your resource library. I am humbled that people find my artwork to their liking. In this book, you have a triple dose of women who are hopelessly committed to the world of dolls. God bless you!

## BARBARA WILLIS

An opportunity to acknowledge and thank friends for this journey is the cherry on top of this book journey. Patti and elinor have been huge inspirations in my life, and I thank them for their friendship, creativity, and their influence. It was a joy to collaborate with these two talented women.

A big thank you to my family who surrounded, encouraged, and cheered me on as I plowed through the details and projects presented in this book. Their critical eyes and kind words kept me on track and moving forward. Love is a wonderful thing.

Quarry Books makes the road smooth and the journey enjoyable—I thank them for all of their help and flexibility. Once again Mary Ann Hall has waved her magic wand and made all things right. Thank you, Mary Ann.

# About the Designers

**elinor peace bailey** graduated as an art major from Brigham Young University. Her focus was painting, but she discovered stitchery while she was raising her large family. She has been traveling and teaching doll making for twenty-six years. During that time elinor has designed fabric for three companies and has been a creative consultant for *Crafts* magazine, has been published frequently in doll-making and quilting magazines. She is the author of *Mother Plays With Dolls, The Rag Doll from Plain to Fancy,* and several additional books. Her self-published works are still available on her website and through quilt shops. She's not finished though, as elinor continues to make dolls, art journals, paintings, quilts and is the shepherdess of her family.

**Patti Medaris Culea** comes to the cloth doll world with a fine arts background. Those skills helped her develop innovative doll designs that are part of her teaching. She travels the world spreading the joy of cloth doll making and offers a full line of cloth doll patterns for those who can't be part of her classes. She is the author of four doll-making books and one on fiber arts, all published by Quarry Books.

**Barbara Willis** is a doll artist and teaches doll making in many parts of the United States, Australia, New Zealand, Canada, and England. Barbara's work has been widely published in magazines, and her dolls have been included in special exhibits, galleries, and books. She loves and collects vintage textiles, and is known for using them in her designs. Barbara resides in Northern California in the San Francisco Bay Area and is the author of *Cloth Doll Artistry* (Quarry Books, 2009).

# Further Reading
## from Quarry Books

*Creative Cloth Doll Making*
Patti Medaris Culea
ISBN 1-56496-942-2

*Creative Cloth Doll Faces*
Patti Medaris Culea
ISBN: 1-59253-144-8

*Creative Cloth Doll Couture*
Patti Medaris Culea
ISBN: 1-59253-217-9

*Creative Cloth Doll Beading*
Patti Medaris Culea
ISBN: 978-1-59253-311-4

*Creative Cloth Explorations*
Patti Medaris Culea
ISBN: 978-1-59253-463-0

*Cloth Doll Artistry*
Barbara Willis
ISBN: 978-1-59253-513-2

*Art Doll Adventures*
Li Hertzi
ISBN: 978-1-59253-267-4

 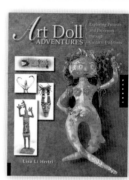

Visit www.Craftside.Typepad.com for a behind-the-scenes peek at our crafty world!